OECD Public Governance Reviews

Towards Efficient Public Procurement in Colombia

MAKING THE DIFFERENCE

This work is published under the responsibility of the Secretary-General of the OECD. The opinions expressed and arguments employed herein do not necessarily reflect the official views of OECD member countries.

This document and any map included herein are without prejudice to the status of or sovereignty over any territory, to the delimitation of international frontiers and boundaries and to the name of any territory, city or area.

Please cite this publication as:
OECD (2016), *Towards Efficient Public Procurement in Colombia: Making the Difference*, OECD Public Governance Reviews, OECD Publishing, Paris.
http://dx.doi.org/10.1787/9789264252103-en

ISBN 978-92-64-25208-0 (print)
ISBN 978-92-64-25210-3 (PDF)

Series: OECD Public Governance Reviews
ISSN 2219-0406 (print)
ISSN 2219-0414 (online)

The statistical data for Israel are supplied by and under the responsibility of the relevant Israeli authorities. The use of such data by the OECD is without prejudice to the status of the Golan Heights, East Jerusalem and Israeli settlements in the West Bank under the terms of international law.

Photo credits: Cover © By Dattis Communications for Colombia Compra Eficiente. Permission granted by Colombia to OECD for reproduction in this publication.

Corrigenda to OECD publications may be found on line at: *www.oecd.org/about/publishing/corrigenda.htm.*

Foreword

Public procurement represents a significant share of countries' economies, on average over 13% of GDP and 29% of government expenditure among OECD members. It is also a rapidly developing field. The combined fiscal pressure to "do more with less" following the financial crisis and the development of new tools and approaches has led to a renaissance in public procurement reform in recent years. The focus of such reform has expanded from enhancing integrity to a broader view of strategic public procurement as way to achieve key government policy objectives, build citizen trust and foster inclusive growth. Countries, including Colombia, are re-evaluating existing processes and procedures to increase efficiency, integrity and service quality, following well-established good governance principles.

While the proportion of GDP attributed to public procurement in Colombia (12.5%) is slightly below the OECD average, public procurement makes up a larger share of government expenditure (35.7%), hence the need to have an improved and robust system. Since 2012, the OECD has worked with Colombia to benchmark and build ownership for ongoing public procurement reforms through collaboration with *Colombia Compra Eficiente* (CCE), which is responsible for developing public procurement policy and expertise in the entire country. Public procurement was recognised as a central element of the National Development Plan, and work has been ongoing to enhance the quality of public-service delivery as well as transparency and accountability in public spending.

The OECD supports governments in reforming their public procurement systems through sharing international good practices, comparative data and conducting peer reviews at the national, sectorial and institutional level. Following an initial evaluation of public procurement in Colombia as part of a 2013 OECD Public Governance Review, CCE invited the OECD to assess the integrity and effectiveness of its procurement system. This report reviews the progress made by CCE by assessing four key areas: public procurement data, management of conflict of interest, contract award procedures and remedy and control systems. Building on good practices identified by the OECD and experiences from other member countries, the peer review also highlights additional steps for advancing the system.

The review recommends measures such as pursuing the development and expansion of a second-generation public procurement information system, reducing duplication by eliminating a mandatory supplier registry that sits outside the e-procurement system, addressing both the policies and management approaches to conflict of interest, making better use of competitive contracting methods to drive competition and efficiency, and streamlining methodologies for legal controls. Developing procurement workforce capacity and implementing reforms at the sub-central level is also essential.

In focusing on continued improvement, CCE demonstrates the benefits of a strategic approach, as public procurement reforms are designed and pursued. This attention to improving results for the government, stakeholders including suppliers, and the citizens as service users demonstrates Colombia's commitment to the OECD mission of designing, developing and delivering better policies for better lives.

Acknowledgements

The OECD expresses its gratitude to *Colombia Compra Eficiente (CCE)* for the invitation to benchmark their ongoing progress in public procurement reform, and for their open dialogue throughout the review process. Under the leadership of Director General Maria Margarita Zuleta, special thanks are offered to the staff of CCE for providing supporting information and facilitating interviews with relevant stakeholders during co-ordination of the peer review process.

As part of a series of peer reviews on public procurement in OECD, G20 and non-member economies, the review benefited from input provided by senior public procurement officials participating in the OECD Meeting of the Working Party of Leading Practitioners on Public Procurement held in Paris on 16-17 December 2015 and chaired by Lorna Prosper, Director General of Defence Procurement and International Cooperation – Public Services and Procurement Canada. Special thanks go to the lead reviewers: Grant Lyons, Acting Chief Information Officer, Ministry of Business, Innovation and Employment, New Zealand; Sašo Matas, General Director, Public Procurement Directorate, Ministry of Public Administration, Slovenia; Guillermo Burr Ortúzar, Head of Research and Business Intelligence, Chile Compra; and Ms. Prosper.

The Review team wishes to acknowledge the significant contribution made by their interlocutors, especially the General Controller Mr. Edgardo Maya Villazón and the heads and members of the several associations of industries and professionals that met with the Review team.

Under the direction of Rolf Alter and János Bertók, this review was led by Paulo Magina, with chapter contributions from Jeremy McCrary, Emma Cantera, Minjoo Son, Petur Matthiasson and Despina Pachnou. Editorial assistance was provided by Thibaut Gigou, Anaisa Goncalves, Pauline Alexandrov and Julie Harris.

Table of contents

Tables

Figures

Acronyms and abbreviations

CCE	*Colombia Compra Eficiente*
CIECI	Construction Industry Ethics and Compliance Initiative
CPACA	*Código de Procedimiento Administrativo y de Contencioso Administrativo*
CPB	Central Purchasing Body
GNC	*Gobierno Nacional Central*
ICT	Information and Communications Technology
NHS	National Health Service
RUP	*Registro Único de Proponentes*
SECOP	*Sistema Electrónico para la Contratación Pública*
SIGEP	*Sistema de Información y Gestión del Empleo Público*
SIIF	*Sistema Integrado de Información*
SMEs	Small and Medium-sized Enterprises
TVEC	*Tienda Virtual del Estado Colombiano*

Executive summary

Public procurement is a crucial activity of government, with important strategic implications. It is not only an area where the public and private spheres intersect; it is also a critical channel for delivering services to citizens. Therefore, ensuring the integrity, transparency and accountability of public procurement is essential to public trust. Providing relevant information to all stakeholders, safeguarding the integrity of officials responsible for the procurement process, opening and levelling the playing field for potential providers, and guaranteeing adequate remedy and redress processes are all cornerstones of an effective public procurement system.

At the same time, the creation of central purchasing bodies (CPBs) as centres of procurement expertise and the development of e-procurement solutions are transforming traditional practices, by sharing knowledge across relevant procurement actors in a more structured way and by enhancing different capabilities across all levels of government, including regional and local counterparts.

In Colombia, public procurement accounts for 12.5% of GDP, slightly below the OECD average, but for a relatively larger share of government expenditure (35.7%). Colombia has recognised the importance of public procurement reforms. *Colombia Compra Eficiente* (CCE) was established in 2012 as the CPB for Colombia and subsequently empowered with a mandate that includes the establishment and operation of framework agreements, responsibility for centralisation and publication of public procurement information, and the development and dissemination of procurement policies and expertise, at both central and sub-national levels.

Key findings

The availability and value of public procurement data have improved, but more can be done to reduce duplication and improve usefulness. The development and expanded use of electronic systems for collecting public procurement information and providing access to framework agreements have improved transparency and efficiency. The transition to the new e-Procurement system (SECOP II) is underway, incorporating key performance indicators. Some avoidable duplication remains, with supplier registration currently required in multiple electronic systems.

The system for identifying, preventing and managing conflict of interest in public procurement could greatly benefit from consolidating the policy framework and implementing a balanced management approach and effective enforcement. While a variety of laws and regulations currently prohibit conflicts of interest and provide sanctions for violation, there is no single national definition, which is a necessary element of a consistent and coherent policy framework.

The extensive use of non-competitive methods for awarding contracts should be addressed to create an open and level playing field for suppliers, as well as to

increase efficiency. Approximately 3 of every 5 contracts in Colombia are awarded through direct contracting, bypassing the benefits of effective competition; the practice is particularly prevalent at the sub-national level. Efforts are underway to improve this outcome through better data collection and analysis, prior planning and market studies, and the expansion of framework agreements. CCE is also taking steps to standardise and protect the bid evaluation process to ensure fairness and transparency.

Legal remedy and control systems are in place, but processes are complicated and focused on compliance with the rules rather than on good commercial outcomes. The public procurement system offers pre-award opportunities for suppliers to offer observations in writing or through hearings, but often these are merely a formality. Litigation is lengthy, with some stakeholders reporting cases lasting up to fifteen years. Fiscal and disciplinary control through the *Contraloría* and the *Procuraduría* can result in substantial financial or judicial sanctions, leading personnel to prioritise risk avoidance over better procurement outcomes.

Key recommendations

To expand the availability and usefulness of public procurement data, CCE should carefully manage the transition to SECOP II, including by publishing information on how it is reducing administrative burdens, thus encouraging additional interest in the use and growth of the system. Building on the good work done in developing key performance indicators, CCE should also look for ways to derive additional value from the data, including developing stakeholder-targeted standardised reports and using it in internal and external efforts to mitigate risks, such as those of the *Contraloría* and the competition authority.

A national definition of conflict of interest should be developed, as well as a specific conflict of interest policy for procurement officials. Adopting positive resolution approaches to managing conflict of interest, including more tailored approaches to asset disclosure or other sources of conflict, can foster an open environment for enhanced integrity. Making such information public also enables the private sector or civil society groups to participate in monitoring activities.

Increasing competition can help improve the climate for awarding contracts. Simplifying and standardising the tendering process would build confidence and support a shift from compliance-based behaviour to more commercially oriented decision making. Sufficient outreach with both procurement agencies and suppliers to disseminate policies, best practices and lessons learned can also support increased competition by levelling the playing field and clarifying expectations, particularly for small and medium-sized enterprises. Additional use of flexible contracting methods such as framework agreements can further reduce the use of direct awarding.

Making maximum use of existing flexibilities can improve redress procedures. For example, potential sources of dispute should be addressed early in the tendering process, such as during the observation and hearings periods. Pre-trial complaint resolution should also be expanded, as this offers real possibilities for assessing and resolving disputes without the burden and disruption of full litigation. A specialised public procurement tribunal for pre-award and contractual disputes could help reduce the case backlog and time delays.

In each of these areas, training, guidance and professionalisation of the public procurement workforce is essential, and will be a necessary condition for the success of the transition to SECOP II. It will also support better use of the data available to procuring entities. Dedicated and systematic integrity training fosters a general climate of integrity and builds confidence in the nature and application of conflict of interest rules among procurement personnel. Proper training in contracting methods and evaluation procedures can support a reduced reliance on direct awarding as well as more consistent and transparent outcomes for suppliers in the awarding process. In all of these areas, ensuring that procurement personnel are aware of the relevant policies, procedures and flexibilities can also support the shift from risk-averse concern for potential complaints to achieving better and more efficient outcomes.

Chapter 1

Harnessing public procurement data in Colombia

The quality, availability and usefulness of data is a key determining factor for the success of public procurement reform. This chapter outlines OECD research on the importance of public procurement data across a number of relevant areas, including an emphasis on transparency, procurement system monitoring, and accountability in the context of the 2015 OECD "Recommendation of the Council on Public Procurement". The important role of e-procurement systems in supporting the collection and use of data is also examined. Against this background, the availability and use of data in the public procurement system in Colombia is explored, with particular focus on the quality of the data collected, real access to the data and opportunities for disclosure among a variety of stakeholders, citizen engagement with public procurement data and related accountability activities.

The statistical data for Israel are supplied by and under the responsibility of the relevant Israeli authorities. The use of such data by the OECD is without prejudice to the status of the Golan Heights, East Jerusalem and Israeli settlements in the West Bank under the terms of international law.

The importance of quality public procurement data

Adequate transparency is central to a well-functioning public procurement system. In monitoring public procurement reforms in OECD countries, "reform efforts [have] focused in particular on ensuring an adequate degree of transparency that does not impede the effectiveness of public procurement" (OECD, 2013a).

This central role of transparency is recognised in the OECD (2015a) "Recommendation of the Council on Public Procurement" (hereafter, the "OECD Recommendation"). See Box 1.1 for the section on transparency in the OECD Recommendation.

Box 1.1. **OECD Recommendation on transparency**

II. RECOMMENDS that Adherents ensure an adequate degree of **transparency** of the public procurement system in all stages of the procurement cycle. To this end, Adherents should:

i) Promote fair and equitable treatment for potential suppliers by providing an adequate and timely degree of transparency in each phase of the public procurement cycle, while taking into account the legitimate needs for protection of trade secrets and proprietary information and other privacy concerns, as well as the need to avoid information that can be used by interested suppliers to distort competition in the procurement process. Additionally, suppliers should be required to provide appropriate transparency in subcontracting relationships.

ii) Allow free access, through an online portal, for all stakeholders, including potential domestic and foreign suppliers, civil society and the general public, to public procurement information notably related to the public procurement system (e.g. institutional frameworks, laws and regulations), the specific procurements (e.g. procurement forecasts, calls for tender, award announcements), and the performance of the public procurement system (e.g. benchmarks, monitoring results). Published data should be meaningful for stakeholder uses.

iii) Ensure visibility of the flow of public funds, from the beginning of the budgeting process throughout the public procurement cycle to allow (i) stakeholders to understand government priorities and spending, and (ii) policy makers to organise procurement strategically.

Source: OECD (2015a), *"Recommendation of the Council on Public Procurement"*, www.oecd.org/corruption/recommendation-on-public-procurement.htm.

As identified in the OECD Recommendation, transparency plays a number of important roles in the public procurement process. Ensuring appropriate transparency into relevant laws, regulations and policies – not to mention public procurement opportunities – sets appropriate expectations and creates a level playing field among suppliers. Transparency into the flow of public funds also allows stakeholders, including the general public, to monitor and evaluate the priorities and effectiveness of government services delivery. From laws and policies through tracking spending, many types of procurement data can be made available. Table 1.1 demonstrates the public availability of these various types of data across OECD countries.

Table 1.1. **Public availability of procurement information at the central level of government**

	Laws and policies	General information for potential bidders	Selection and evaluation criteria	Contract award	Specific guidance on application procedures	Tender documents	Procurement plan of anticipated tenders	Justification for awarding contract to selected contractor	Contract modifications	Tracking procurement spending
Australia	●	□	□	●	□	□	●	■	□	●
Austria	●	□	□	□	□	□	□	○	□	○
Belgium	●	●	●	●	●	●	●	●	●	○
Canada	●	●	■	●	●	■	○	■	●	○
Chile	●	●	□	●	●	●	●	●	□	●
Czech Republic	●	●	●	●	●	●	□	□	□	□
Denmark	●	●	□	□	□	□	●	□	□	○
Estonia	●	●	●	●	●	■	●	●	■	●
Finland	●	●	●	●	□	■	□	●	○	○
France	●	●	●	□	●	□	□	■	●	■
Germany	●	●	□	□	○	□	○	○	○	○
Greece	●	●	●	●	□	●	□	●	○	○
Hungary	●	●	●	●	●	●	●	●	●	●
Iceland	●	●	●	●	●	●	●	●	●	■
Ireland	●	●	●	□	□	●	●	□	□	○
Israel	●	□	●	□	□	●	□	■	●	○
Italy	●	●	●	●	●	●	●	■	●	■
Japan	●	●	●	●	●	●	●	●	●	■
Korea	●	●	●	●	●	●	●	●	●	●
Luxembourg	●	●	●	□	□	●	□	■	■	□
Mexico	●	●	●	●	●	●	●	●	□	●
Netherlands	●	□	□	□	□	□	□	□	□	○
New Zealand	●	■	●	●	■	●	●	■	■	○
Norway	●	□	□	□	□	■	●	■	■	■
Poland	●	●	●	●	●	●	●	●	■	○
Portugal	●	□	□	□	□	□	□	□	□	□
Slovak Republic	●	●	●	●	●	■	□	○	●	○
Slovenia	●	□	□	□	□	□	□	■	□	■
Spain	●	●	●	●	●	●	●	●	●	○
Sweden	●	●	□	□	●	□	□	□	○	○
Switzerland	●	●	●	●	●	●	○	●	○	□
Turkey	●	●	●	●	●	●	□	■	■	●
United Kingdom	●	●	○	●	●	○	●	□	○	○
United States	●	●	□	□	□	□	□	○	■	□
Brazil	●	●	●	●	■	●	○	■	●	●
Egypt	●	●	●	□	●	●	○	○	□	○
Ukraine	●	●	●	●	●	●	●	■	○	○
Total OECD34										
● Always	34	26	21	21	19	18	17	13	11	7
■ Upon request	0	1	1	0	1	5	0	10	7	6
□ Sometimes	0	7	11	13	13	10	14	7	10	5
○ Not available	0	0	1	0	1	1	3	4	6	16

Source: OECD (2013a), *Implementing the OECD Principles for Integrity in Public Procurement: Progress since 2008*, OECD Public Governance Reviews, OECD Publishing, Paris, http://dx.doi.org/10.1787/9789264201385-en.

Note: The statistical data for Israel are supplied by and under the responsibility of the relevant Israeli authorities. The use of such data by the OECD is without prejudice to the status of the Golan Heights, East Jerusalem and Israeli settlements in the West Bank under the terms of international law.

At the same time, increasing transparency was identified by governments as a substantial area for improvement in an OECD survey (see Figure 1.1).

Figure 1.1. **Areas for improvement in procurement management**

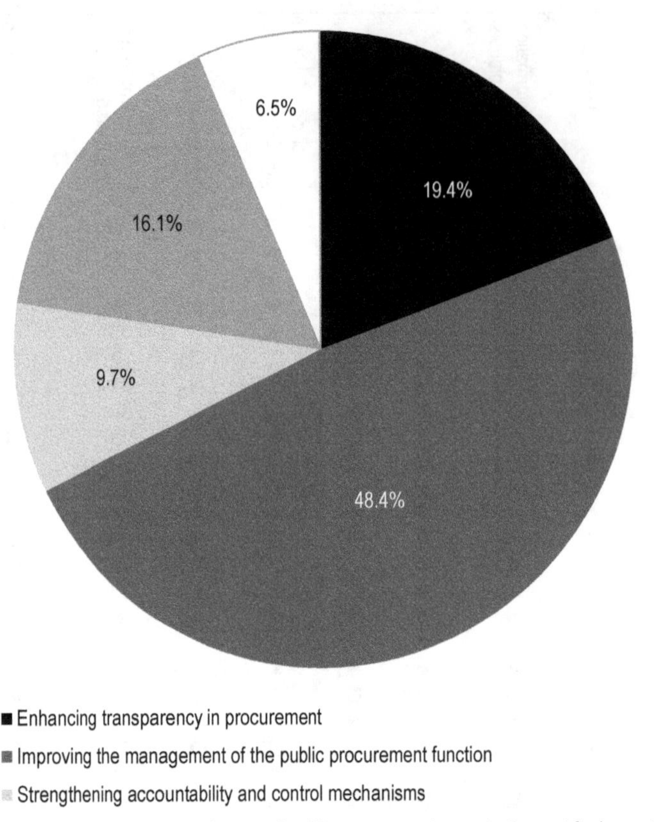

■ Enhancing transparency in procurement
■ Improving the management of the public procurement function
■ Strengthening accountability and control mechanisms
■ Developing guidance on the use of public procurement as an instrument for innovation
□ Other

Source: OECD (2013a), *Implementing the OECD Principles for Integrity in Public Procurement: Progress since 2008*, OECD Public Governance Reviews, OECD Publishing, Paris, http://dx.doi.org/10.1787/9789264201385-en.

Similarly, transparency and access to data were identified as key concerns by external stakeholders in a recent survey related to the development of a major infrastructure project, the New International Airport in Mexico City (see Box 1.2).

Beyond the importance of transparency, the OECD Recommendation also highlights the importance of quality public procurement data in driving performance improvements. Accurate data regarding individual purchases is important for monitoring the health and function of the public procurement system. When aggregated and developed into performance indicators, such data can support substantial reforms to increase efficiency and eliminate waste in the public procurement process (see Box 1.3).

Additionally, reliable public procurement data, presented in appropriate forms, is of critical importance in ensuring appropriate accountability in the public procurement system (see Box 1.4).

Box 1.2. **Top concerns expressed by non-governmental organisations (NGOs) in relation to the development of the New International Airport in Mexico City**

Transparency and trust. Communications and outreach efforts have to be more systematic and proactive in order to create and reinforce trust.

Mechanisms of access to public records. More technical studies and financial projections need to be available for public scrutiny.

Financial sustainability. The fall in oil prices will inevitably lead to cuts in public budgets. There are concerns about the availability of government resources to pay for the project given the Government's austerity measures.

Timetable and execution capability. The Government is seen as optimistic in its assertions that the airport will be ready by 2020.

Urban mobility plans. NGO leaders believe that the mobility plans are not in place, and they should have been ready before construction started.

Surrounding communities. Negotiations with local social leaders could foster distrust. Openness, consultation, and dialogue with local communities would better serve the Government's efforts to prevent conflicts.

Political conflict. As the 2018 elections come closer, changes in the political landscape could evidently put additional pressure on the project. The future use of the current airport also looms as a potential disagreement between the city and federal authorities.

Public security. The authorities seemed to have overlooked the fact that the *Nuevo Aeropuerto Internacional de la Ciudad de México* (NAICM) will be located in a high-crime area. Plans for regional security are needed.

Air safety. Some specialists consider that the area poses challenges that need to be fully addressed to ensure air safety. Birds are the top concern, and special measures will need to be taken.

Inter-institutional co-ordination. NGO leaders perceive that agencies such as CONAGUA, SEDATU, and SEMARNAT are not exactly on the same page as the SCT and GACM.

Source: OECD (2015b), *Effective Delivery of Large Infrastructure Projects: The Case of the New International Airport of Mexico City*, OECD Public Governance Reviews, OECD Publishing, Paris, http://dx.doi.org/10.1787/9789264248335-en.

Box 1.3. **OECD Recommendation on evaluation**

X. RECOMMENDS that Adherents drive performance improvements through **evaluation** of the effectiveness of the public procurement system from individual procurements to the system as a whole, at all levels of government where feasible and appropriate. To this end, Adherents should:

i) Assess periodically and consistently the results of the procurement process. Public procurement systems should collect consistent, up-to-date and reliable information and use data on prior procurements, particularly regarding price and overall costs, in structuring new needs assessments, as they provide a valuable source of insight and could guide future procurement decisions.

ii) Develop indicators to measure performance, effectiveness and savings of the public procurement system for benchmarking and to support strategic policy making on public procurement.

Source: OECD (2015a), *"Recommendation of the Council on Public Procurement"*, www.oecd.org/corruption/recommendation-on-public-procurement.htm.

Box 1.4. **OECD Recommendation on accountability**

XII. RECOMMENDS that Adherents apply oversight and control mechanisms to support **accountability** throughout the public procurement cycle, including appropriate complaint and sanctions processes.

To this end, Adherents should:

…

iv) Ensure that internal controls (including financial controls, internal audit and management controls), and external controls and audits are co-ordinated, sufficiently resourced and integrated to ensure:

1. the monitoring of the performance of the public procurement system;
2. the reliable reporting and compliance with laws and regulations as well as clear channels for reporting credible suspicions of breaches of those laws and regulations to the competent authorities, without fear of reprisals;
3. the consistent application of procurement laws, regulations and policies;
4. a reduction of duplication and adequate oversight in accordance with national choices; and
5. independent *ex post* assessment and, where appropriate, reporting to relevant oversight bodies.

Source: OECD (2015a), *"Recommendation of the Council on Public Procurement"*, www.oecd.org/corruption/recommendation-on-public-procurement.htm.

In support of expanded transparency, evaluation and accountability, the use of digital technology to support procurement processes has been adopted by many countries. In their most straightforward application, e-procurement tools have the potential to dramatically increase efficiency by eliminating wasteful and duplicative paper-based processes. Beyond this, e-procurement tools can also play a transformative role by enabling processes that are simply impossible to replicate without advanced digital technologies. This dual potential is therefore identified in the OECD Recommendation's definition of e-procurement as "the integration of digital technologies in the replacement or redesign of paper-based procedures throughout the procurement process." Through proper application, e-procurement systems also improve automation and standardisation, reducing time to complete tasks and the probability of human error, which is important for obtaining quality public procurement data. For these reasons, adoption of e-procurement is an important element of the OECD Recommendation (see Box 1.5).

Within this framework, the next sections explore the current state of e-procurement and public procurement data in Colombia, looking to recent improvements, ongoing efforts and recommendations for future directions.

Box 1.5. **OECD Recommendation on e-procurement**

VIII. RECOMMENDS that Adherents improve the public procurement system by harnessing the use of digital technologies to support appropriate **e-procurement** innovation throughout the procurement cycle.

To this end, Adherents should:

i) Employ recent digital technology developments that allow integrated e-procurement solutions covering the procurement cycle. Information and communication technologies should be used in public procurement to ensure transparency and access to public tenders, increasing competition, simplifying processes for contract award and management, driving cost savings and integrating public procurement and public finance information.

ii) **Pursue state-of-the-art e-procurement tools that are modular, flexible, scalable and secure** in order to assure business continuity, privacy and integrity, provide fair treatment and protect sensitive data, while supplying the core capabilities and functions that allow business innovation. E-procurement tools should be simple to use and appropriate to their purpose, and consistent across procurement agencies, to the extent possible; excessively complicated systems could create implementation risks and challenges for new entrants or small and medium-sized enterprises.

Source: OECD (2015a), *"Recommendation of the Council on Public Procurement"*, www.oecd.org/corruption/recommendation-on-public-procurement.htm.

SECOP and SECOP II: Progress in improving data collection

SECOP

As a result of the implementation of law 1150/2007, the *Sistema Electrónico para la Contratación Pública* (SECOP) was created as an initial e-procurement system. SECOP exists primarily for contract publishing and also includes notices and information on awards. Government agencies are required to publish all procurement activity under Article 19 of Decree 1510 (2013), with the definition of procurement documents and an indicative list provided in Article 3 of the same decree. This includes:

- studies and prior documents related to the contract
- the call for tender
- statements of conditions for the invitation
- any addendums
- the offer
- the evaluation report
- the contract
- any other document issued by the entity during the contracting process.

Government agencies are also required to annually publish an acquisition plan on SECOP in a specified format, providing insights into future government needs.

As noted in the report on the procurement review conducted as part of the previous public governance review of Colombia, SECOP "makes procurement information easily available and helps bidders find procurement opportunities and authorities find procurement-related information" (OECD, 2013b). In fact, implementation of SECOP led to a 286% increase in the value of procurement information publicly available between 2011 and 2014. However, as the report identifies, there are issues which limit the effectiveness of SECOP.

First, data is manually entered into SECOP, not through connection to originating systems or through imported electronic files. This creates an opportunity for delay and inaccuracy, and in practice SECOP contains omissions and mistakes. To address this shortcoming, *Colombia Compra Eficiente* (CCE) undertakes an annual revision of the records made by all agencies to identify inconsistencies and ask for corrections. This method addresses some of the concern, but it is resource intensive and limited in scope, as the review covers only a sample of the available records (though the sample is large, with 45 000 records in 2014). This shortcoming is also addressed, to some extent, by participation of the market, when external stakeholders question available information or request that information be updated for accuracy.

Next, the data available in SECOP is not presented in a form that provides for structured extraction. CCE currently undertakes efforts to provide the number of contracts entered without competitive process, the number of offers submitted in each selection process, and any data required for the procurement accountability functions of the Inspector General of Colombia (*Procuraduría General de la Nación*, the *Procuraduría*) and the Comptroller General's Office (*Contraloria General de la República*, the *Contraloria*). Because all such data and outputs must be manually processed, CCE must dedicate time and resources to structuring the information in SECOP into a usable form for these and other stakeholders.

Finally, SECOP does not interface with other sources of information relevant to the procurement process. The Single Suppliers Register (*Registro Único de Proponentes*, RUP), operated by the Association of Chambers of Commerce (*Confecámaras)*, is the source of registry for suppliers wishing to participate in public procurement activities, but it does not connect directly to link certifications in SECOP. Similarly, the Financial Information Integrated System (*Sistema Integrado de Información Financiera*, SIIF) is not integrated to connect budget, accounting and procurement information.

SECOP II

To address these issues, CCE has designed and implemented a next-generation e-procurement platform, SECOP II. Designed to increase electronic availability of all procurement documents, allow electronic communication at all stages of the procurement cycle, and allow electronic submission of tenders. By expanding the functionalities for e-procurement, Colombia is in line with many OECD countries. As of 2014, all OECD member countries announce procurement opportunities and provide tender documents through their e-procurement systems; most of these countries are mandated by law to provide these functionalities. Functionalities at the beginning of the procurement cycle - in particular publishing of procurement plans (86%), electronic submission of bids (90%), and e-tendering (86%) - are provided in most OECD countries. In contrast, those towards the end of procurement cycle (except for notification of award [97%]) are provided by a lower number of OECD member countries. Fewer countries provide e-auctions, ordering, electronic submission of invoices and *ex post* contract management through their e-procurement systems. The majority of countries provide these functionalities in their e-procurement systems even though they are not obliged by law (see Table 1.2).

Table 1.2. **Functionalities of e-procurement systems**

	Mandatory and provided	Not mandatory but provided	Not provided
Publishing procurement plans (about forecasted government needs)	AUS, BEL, CHL, DMK, GRC, HUN, IRL, KOR, MEX, NZL, NOR, PRT, GBR, USA	AUT, CAN, FIN, DEU, ITA, JPN, POL, SVN, ESP, SWE, CHE	EST, FRA, LUX, SVK
Announcing tenders	AUS, AUT, BEL, CAN, CHL, DNK, EST, FIN, FRA, DEU, GRC, HUN, IRL, ITA, KOR, LUX, MEX, NZL, NOR, POL, PRT, SVK, SVN, ESP, SWE, CHE, GBR, USA	JPN	
Provision of tender documents	AUS, AUT, BEL, CHL, EST, FIN, FRA, DEU, GRC, HUN, IRL, KOR, MEX, NZL, NOR, POL, PRT, SVK, SVN, SWE, CHE, GBR, USA	CAN, DNK, ITA, JPN, LUX, ESP	
Electronic submission of bids (excluding by e-mails)	BEL, CHL, EST, FRA, GRC, ITA, MEX, PRT, USA	AUS, AUT, CAN, DNK, FIN, DEU, IRL, JPN, KOR, LUX, NZL, NOR, SVK, SVN, ESP, SWE, GBR	HUN, POL, CHE
E-tendering	BEL, CAN, CHL, EST, GRC, IRL, ITA, MEX, CHE, USA	AUT, DNK, FIN, FRA, DEU, JPN, KOR, NZL, NOR, PRT, SVK, SVN, ESP, SWE, GBR	AUS, HUN, LUX, POL
E-auctions (in e-tendering)	GRC, MEX, SVK, SVN, USA	DNK, EST, FIN, FRA, DEU, IRL, ITA, NZL, NOR, PRT, SWE, CHE, GBR	AUS, AUT, BEL, CAN, CHL, HUN, JPN, KOR, LUX, POL, ESP
Notification of award	AUT, BEL, CAN, CHL, DNK, EST, FIN, DEU, GRC, HUN, IRL, KOR, MEX, NZL, NOR, POL, PRT, SVK, SVN, ESP, SWE, CHE, USA	AUS, FRA, ITA, JPN, GBR	LUX
Ordering	CHL, FIN, ITA, CHE, USA	AUT, BEL, CAN, DNK, FRA, DEU, JPN, KOR, NZL, NOR, SVN, ESP, SWE, GBR	AUS, EST, GRC, HUN, IRL, LUX, MEX, POL, PRT, SVK
Electronic submission of invoices (excluding by e-mails)	AUT, DNK, FIN, ITA, ESP, SVN, SWE, CHE, USA	FRA, DEU, JPN, KOR, NZL, NOR, GBR	AUS, BEL, CAN, CHL, EST, GRC, HUN, IRL, LUX, MEX, POL, PRT, SVK
Ex post contract management	CHE, USA	AUT, DNK, FIN, DEU, ITA, JPN, KOR, NZL, NOR, SWE	AUS, BEL, CAN, CHL, EST, FRA, GRC, HUN, IRL, LUX, MEX, POL, PRT, SVK, SVN, ESP, GBR

Source: OECD (2015c), *Government at a Glance 2015*, OECD Publishing, Paris, http://dx.doi.org/10.1787/gov_glance-2015-en.

SECOP II is currently in the early stages of deployment. To ensure a successful transition, CCE has published drafts of the user manuals for SECOP II addressed to both government agencies and the private sector, and has designed training courses to teach the use of the system. There is an ambitious goal to bring on board 4 076 government agencies as users by 2018, including all national and department procuring entities as well as the mayors of major cities. State-owned businesses are currently instructed by CCE Circular 20 and related guidance to provide links to SECOP. Such entities will be encouraged to use SECOP II, but not required by law to do so; some such as the City of Bogota Water Supply Company are already committed to doing so. In order to attract users that are not mandated to use the system, CCE should develop metrics for analysing burden reduction associated with the move to new electronic processes made possible by SECOP II.

As with any major transition, change management will be an important element of a successful implementation of SECOP II. Adoption of e-procurement brings with it specific challenges, and the OECD has identified these common challenges faced by countries in order to be addressed successfully. When responding to the OECD Survey on Public Procurement, the main challenge faced by both procuring entities and potential bidders and suppliers with regard to using e-procurement systems was limited knowledge and information and communications technology (ICT) skills (48%). This issue must be addressed through training and development of the procurement workforce. Low innovative organisational culture (41%) and limited knowledge of the economic opportunities raised by e-procurement systems (32%) were identified as additional challenges for procuring entities. Related to potential bidders and suppliers, 12 OECD member countries (41%) identified difficulties in understanding or applying the procedures and difficulties in the use of the functionalities as additional challenges (see Table 1.3). In addition, the broad geographical spread in Colombia will be a challenge to incorporating all of the targeted procuring entities.

Toward reliable and useful data

In addition to providing increased functionality and broader coverage of the public procurement cycle, one of the most important advantages of SECOP II will be the automation and centralisation of many of the data collection activities. By collecting data in structured formats, the resource-intensive processes of manually reporting data, manually sampling and testing for inaccuracies, and manually generating relevant reporting from the system can be eliminated, and these resources dedicated to other functions within the context of improving the public procurement system.

As the system was developed, Colombia recognised the importance of developing key performance indicators that can be derived from information available from within SECOP II and other related systems. Eleven key indicators across four key target areas have been identified and defined, and baseline evaluations have been conducted (see Box 1.6). These efforts are consistent with other countries identification of relevant information on which to base performance indicators for the health of the procurement system (see Box 1.7), as well as with ongoing OECD work to define and develop key performance indicators.

Table 1.3. **Challenges faced in e-procurement implementation**

	Procuring entities				Potential bidders/suppliers					
	Limited knowledge/ ICT skills	Limited knowledge of the economic opportunities raised by this tool	Low innovative organisational culture	Do not know	Limited knowledge/ ICT skills	Limited knowledge of the economic opportunities raised by this tool	Difficulties understanding or applying the procedure	Difficulties in the use of functionalities (e.g. catalogue management)	Low propensity to innovation	Do not know
Australia	No major challenges faced by procuring entities				No major challenges faced by potential bidders/suppliers					
Austria				●						●
Belgium			●						●	
Canada	●				●	●	●	●	●	
Chile				●		●	●	●		
Denmark				●			●	●		
Estonia		●				●				
Finland				●						●
France				●						●
Germany	●	●	●			●		●		
Greece		●	●		●	●			●	
Hungary	●		●		●		●	●		
Ireland				●			●			
Italy	●		●		●		●	●	●	
Japan	●	●			●	●	●	●		
Korea	●		●		●				●	
Luxembourg				●						●
Mexico	●	●	●							●
New Zealand	●	●			●	●				
Norway		●				●	●		●	
Poland	●		●		●		●	●		
Portugal	●				●		●			
Slovak Republic		●			●			●		
Slovenia	●	●	●		●	●	●	●	●	
Spain		●	●		●	●			●	
Sweden				●						●
Switzerland				●						●
United Kingdom	●		●			●		●		
United States	●		●		●		●	●	●	
Brazil	●	●	●		●	●	●	●		
Colombia	●	●	●		●	●			●	
OECD 29	13	10	12	9	13	11	12	12	9	7

Source: OECD (2015c), *Government at a Glance 2015*, OECD Publishing, Paris, http://dx.doi.org/10.1787/gov_glance-2015-en.

Box 1.6. Indicators to measure the national procurement system

Indicator	What does it measure?	Description
Value for money		
Opportunity of the contracting process	The level of budgetary commitments in a fiscal year	Ratio between the commitments and the appropriation during the fiscal year, which does not include staff costs, budgetary transferences, and debt expenses
Changes in value according to specifications	The variation in the value of the contracts between the initial value established in the tender documents and the final value awarded	Average difference between the estimated value for the selection and the final value of the contract
Average time of the selection process according to the award mechanism	Difference in time of the selection process by award mechanism	Period of time between the signature date of a contract and the starting date of the process
Integrity and transparency in competition		
Average of new contractors	Percentage of new contractors in a public entity regarding the former year	Ratio of new contractors of a public entity regarding the number of contractors working in the public entity in the previous year
Concentration of the contracts' value by contractor	The concentration of resources by contractor that perform for a public entity through public procurement	Concentration of a public entity's budget by contractor measured by the Gini coefficient
Percentage of contracts awarded to plural bidders	Frequency of awarded contracts to plural bidders by a public entity	Ratio of the contracts and the value of the contracts awarded by a public entity to plural bidders
Percentage of contracts awarded in non-competitive processes	Percentage of public contracting that is done under non-competitive processes	Percentage of awarded contracts without a competitive process, not including inter-administrative contracts, reserve spending of the defence sector and professional services
Accountability		
Percentage of public entity users of SECOP	SECOP use by the public entities that are obligated to use it	Percentage of public entities using SECOP
Percentage of public entities that publish their annual acquisition plans on SECOP	The progress in the compliance of the publication of the Annual Acquisition Plan on SECOP	Percentage of public entities that publish every year their Annual Acquisition Plan on SECOP
Percentage of publicity of the contracting processes in SECOP	The level of publication on SECOP of the contracts signed in a fiscal year	Percentage of the value of the procurement processes that a public entity publishes on SECOP
Risk management		
Percentage of contracts with modifications in time and/or value	Proportion of contracts modified after their signature regarding the total of contracts done by a public entity	Proportion of contracts modified in the value or in the duration of their performance after their signature

Box 1.6. **Indicators to measure the national procurement system** *(continued)*

In 2015, *Colombia Compra Eficiente* made the first indicators estimation of the Public Procurement System using the procurement information of the State Entities in 2014. The baseline results are presented in the following table.

Dimension	Indicator	Results baseline (2014)
Value for money	Opportunity of the contracting processes	7.4%
	Changes in value according to specifications	0.1%
	Average time of the selection process according to the award mechanism	Open tender: 37 days
		Merit contest: 38 days
		Abbreviated selection: 37 days
		Reverse auction: 38 days
		Abbreviated selection in instruments to aggregate demand: 9 days
		Direct contracting: 26 days
		Special regime: 38 days
		Selection with small budget: 12 days
		Lower value: 38 days
Integrity and transparency in competition	Average of new contractors	24.1%
	Concentration of the contracts' value by contractor	0.638
	Percentage of contracts awarded to plural bidders	10%
	Percentage of contracts awarded in non-competitive processes	38.5%
Accountability	Percentage of public entities users of SECOP	99%
	Percentage of public entities that publish their annual acquisition plan on SECOP	58%
	Percentage of publicity of the contracting processes in SECOP	49%
Risk management	Percentage of contracts with modifications in time or value	23%

Source: Information provided by CCE.

Additionally, SECOP II is integrated with the SIIF financial information system. In implementation of the *Tienda Virtual del Estado Colombiano* – the e-store system for the framework agreements managed by CCE – work was done to integrate with SIIF, and the development of SECOP II has benefited from this experience. A remaining challenge will be to integrate SECOP II with the financial systems at the subnational level. By providing a direct connection with the financial reporting system, data accuracy and transparency into the spending of procurement entities is much advanced.

Box 1.7. Establishing good key performance indicators

Good key performance indicators must possess some fundamental qualities to fully benefit an organisation and its suppliers. They should be:

- **Relevant**, i.e. linked to key objectives of the organisation (critical outcomes or risks to be avoided), rather than on process.
- **Clear**, i.e. spelled out in the contractual document and as simple as possible to ensure common understanding by the buying organisation and the supplier.
- **Measurable and objective**, i.e. expressed on pre-determined measures and formulas, and based on simple data that can be gathered objectively and in a cost-effective manner.
- **Achievable**, i.e. realistic and within the control of the supplier.
- **Limited**, i.e. as few as required achieving the objectives while minimising their disadvantages (costs, efforts and risk of dispute) to both entities. To the extent possible, the use of information and documentation already available under the contract management process should be promoted rather than requiring the collection of additional data or documentation.
- **Timed**, i.e. include specific timeframes for completion.

Procurement key performance indicators can be established for any important objective of the organisation. While a wide variety of subjects can be considered, the following ones may be appropriate:

- **Delivery**, i.e. whether the supplier delivers on time, delivers the right items and quantities, provides accurate documentation and information, responds to emergency delivery requirements, etc.
- **Pricing**: competitiveness, price stability, volume or other discounts, etc.
- **Customer service**: number of product shortages due to the supplier, training provided on equipment and products, warranty services, administrative efficiency (including order acknowledgement and accurate invoice), accuracy of performance data and reports provided by the suppliers, etc.
- **Product**: meets specifications (including percentage of rejects/defects), reliability/durability under usage, packaging, quality and availability of documentation and technical manuals, etc.

Finally, not all key performance indicators have to be monitored on the same frequency, the majority potentially being assessed on a monthly basis, with others only quarterly or even annually.

Source: OECD (2013c), *Public Procurement Review of the State's Employees' Social Security and Social Services Institute in Mexico*, OECD Public Governance Reviews, OECD Publishing, Paris, http://dx.doi.org/10.1787/9789264197305-en.

The situation regarding the relation between SECOP II and RUP is somewhat more complicated. Under current law, RUP is the mandated database for registration of supplier information. However, there are some challenges related to this arrangement. The fact-finding mission identified issues related to the cost and burden of registration in RUP. Suppliers are required to submit substantial documentation to register within RUP. Additionally, registration is required on an annual basis; if a supplier fails to register within the appropriate time frame, they are automatically removed from the system. Finally, there is a cost to register with RUP, currently approximately USD 64. While this cost is not prohibitive, some stakeholders expressed concern that the overall cost and burden together is a reason why some suppliers resist attempting to provide goods and services to the government in Colombia. There are currently only 33 000 registered suppliers within RUP, which is a very small fraction of total potential suppliers in Colombia.

SECOP II includes an independent supplier registration process, which is also required for participating in the additional functionalities provided by the new system, including bidding on contracts conducted electronically. This registration is free for suppliers, but is therefore duplicative with the RUP process. While the RUP system offers some additional benefits, including verification by the Chambers of Commerce of the information submitted by suppliers, Colombia should consider options for addressing this duplication of effort in a manner that reduces costs and burdens for suppliers. Such efforts to streamline multiple data sources to reduce duplication have been ongoing in some OECD countries, such as the United States (see Box 1.8).

Box 1.8. **Consolidation of suppliers' information in the United States**

The System for Award Management (SAM, www.sam.gov) is a US Federal Government owned and operated free website that consolidates the capabilities from various legacy databases and systems used in federal procurement and awards processes. As it relates to suppliers' information, it covers the following systems:

- The Central Contractor Registration (CCR) is the Federal Government's primary vendor database that collects, validates, stores, and disseminates vendor data in support of agency acquisition missions. Both current and potential vendors are required to register in the CCR to be eligible for federal contracts. Once vendors are registered, their data are shared with other federal electronic business systems that promote the paperless communication and co-operation between systems. The information and capabilities of CCR are gradually being transferred into SAM.
- The Excluded Parties Lists System (EPLS) was a web-based system that identified parties excluded from receiving federal contracts, certain subcontracts, and certain types of federal financial and non-financial assistance and benefits. The EPLS was updated to reflect government-wide administrative and statutory exclusions, and also included suspected terrorists and individuals barred from entering the United States. The user was able to search, view, and download current and archived exclusions. All the exclusion capabilities of the EPLS were transferred to SAM in November 2012.

Furthermore, federal agencies are required since July 2009 to post all contractor performance evaluations on the Past Performance Information Retrieval System (PPIRS, www.ppirs.gov). That web-based, government-wide application provides timely and pertinent information on a contractor's past performance to the federal acquisition community for making source selection decisions. PPIRS provides a query capability for authorised users to retrieve report card information detailing a contractor's past performance. Federal regulations require that report cards be completed annually by customers during the life of the contract. The PPIRS consists of several sub-systems and databases (e.g. Contractor Performance System, Past Performance Data Base, and Construction Contractor Appraisal Support System).

Source: OECD (2013b), *Colombia: Implementing Good Governance*, OECD Public Governance Reviews, OECD Publishing, Paris, http://dx.doi.org/10.1787/9789264202177-en.

Focusing on stakeholders

In all of its work, CCE recognises the importance of providing relevant information to a wide variety of stakeholders. Previous efforts have included the development of an RSS feed to help the private sector identify public procurement opportunities, providing data as requested to the *Procuraduría* and *Contraloría* as required for oversight activities, developed and released the *Síntesis* system to consult legal and jurisprudential information related to public procurement, opened a help desk for all stakeholder, offered manuals and videos for the use of electronic systems, and issued manuals and guides designed to further understanding of the function of the procurement system. CCE also publishes a regular bulletin designed to highlight ongoing efforts and improvements for interested stakeholders. The implementation of SECOP II provides a number of opportunities to continue and expand this trend of stakeholder engagement.

As with any public procurement system, this outreach targets a number of relevant stakeholder groups. Government purchasing entities, suppliers and potential suppliers, control authorities, the media and NGOs and the general public all have a high degree of interest in receiving targeted and relevant outputs from the public procurement system. Through interviews with stakeholders from these various groups, the fact-finding mission identified an appreciation of the efforts undertaken by CCE so far, as well as substantial interest and anticipation in working together to implement SECOP II.

Government entities, suppliers and industry stakeholder groups who were interviewed expressed a strong interest in the reduced burden that will come from transforming many current processes into electronic processes, and the only consistently expressed concern involved a desire to move more quickly into adoption of SECOP II. Many also expressed the view that the move to SECOP II and more clearly defined electronic processes will help to eliminate some of the barriers that potential new entrants have in understanding the public procurement process.

Both the *Procuraduría* and *Contraloría* expressed satisfaction with the interaction with CCE regarding data necessary to carry out their functions. Both entities also welcome the additional possibilities available with SECOP II, including a suggestion from the *Contraloría* to better integrate public procurement information into the development of risk matrices used to evaluate the sufficiency of processes and the efficiency of outcomes. One recommendation for future action in this area involves the development of a feedback loop, designed to share findings of problems to inform future policy development and training.

Journalists are also heavy users of public procurement information currently provided by SECOP and CCE. Stakeholder interviews expressed surprise and satisfaction at the amount of information made available by CCE, and also with the availability of CCE personnel to address questions regarding whether data was available, or why it was not. As with other stakeholder groups, anticipation of the benefits involved in the transition to SECOP II was expressed. Both improved quality and better interconnection of the data available were highlighted as benefits of the new system. Additionally, the timeliness of available information was cited as of critical concern for the stakeholders that were interviewed.

Within this context, CCE can consider the development of additional standard reporting elements that can further satisfy stakeholder needs. While standard and automated reporting for the health and function of the procurement system is already planned, the available data can also be packaged in more targeted ways. Some state-of-the-art country procurement systems have begun to add this functionality, as in the example of Korea (see Box 1.9).

Box 1.9. **Korea's public procurement data system**

While almost 70% of public procurement transactions in Korea occur via the Korean ON-line E-Procurement System (KONEPS), the remaining transactions, including defence procurement, procurement transactions by other public enterprises that use their own e-procurement systems and some manual transactions, are not currently captured in a centralised way. In 2013, Korea's Public Procurement Service (PPS) launched a Public Procurement Data System project to close this gap and provide policy makers and citizens with complete procurement transaction data across the entire public sector, enabling a better understanding of the procurement market and an analytical study on the policy results.

Proper legal authority for the project was established by the modifications of procurement laws including the Government Procurement Act (July 2013) and the Enforcement Decree on the Government Procurement Act (January 2014), giving PPS the legal authority to request data and establishing deadlines for government agencies to submit the requested procurement data.

Total public procurement encompasses procurements that occur in both electronic and non-electronic ways. Electronic procurement is carried out on KONEPS and 23 other electronic procurement platforms for specific procuring entities. Thus, data integration includes linking of the 24 e-procurement systems as well as central collection of manual records. A report will be prepared to present the data collected per government bodies, companies, and projects. Data will also be presented in infographics in order to facilitate end user comprehension.

The data integration faces some difficulties due to administrative burdens that are imposed on approximately 28 000 government agencies and delays in concomitant projects in some government agencies to improve their electronic systems, which were intended to facilitate the data integration. In order to alleviate the administrative burden on the collection of manually kept data, discussion on linking with other financial information systems is taking place, including the Educational Financial System, the Local Government Budget and Accounting System, the Local Pubic Enterprise Budget and Accounting System and the National Budget and Accounting System. Additionally, some difficulties arose due to the disparity of the information collected at each government agency and across different e-procurement systems. In response, new code mapping was provided to agencies where data were collected by different standards.

Provision and publication of data statistics on total public procurement on a monthly and annual basis and 103 specific reports based on the data are expected to increase availability of the data for companies and the public, and enhance transparency of the government budget. The reports will be made available on line.

Source: OECD (2016), *The Korean Public Procurement Service: Innovating for Effectiveness*, OECD Public Governance Reviews, OECD Publishing, Paris, http://dx.doi.org/10.1787/9789264249431-en.

Future directions

In addition to the planned activities designed to better utilise public procurement data available in SECOP II, there are additional methods of data integration that should be considered for future implementation.

Risk management

The availability of real-time, quality public procurement information regarding ongoing activities provides an opportunity to develop risk-management tools that are otherwise unavailable. In many countries, such systems are being designed to provide "red flags" during ongoing procurement processes as a means of highlighting cases where additional investigation may be required. Examples include the Public Spending Observatory established in Brazil (see Box 1.10) and the National Database on Public Contracts established in Italy (see Box 1.11).

Box 1.10. **Brazil's Public Spending Observatory**

The Office of the Comptroller General of the Union launched the Public Spending Observatory (*Observatório da Despesa Pública*) in 2008 as the basis for continuous detection and sanctioning of misconduct and corruption. Through the Public Spending Observatory, procurement expenditure data are cross-checked with other government databases as a means of identifying atypical situations that, while not *a priori* evidence of irregularities, warrant further examination.

Based on the experience over the past several years, a number of daily actions are taken to cross procurement and other government data. This exercise generates "orange" or "red" flags that can be followed up and investigated by officials within the Office of the Comptroller General of the Union. In many cases, follow-up activities are conducted together with special Advisors on Internal Control and internal audit units within public organisations.

Examples of these tracks related to procurement and administrative contracts include possible conflicts of interest, inappropriate use of exemptions and waivers and substantial contract amendments. A number of tracks also relate to suspicious patterns of bid rotation and market division among competitors by sector, geographic area or time, which might indicate that bidders are acting in a collusive scheme.

Finally, tracks also exist regarding the use of federal government payment cards and administrative agreements (*convenios*). In 2013, there were 60 000 instances of warnings originated from the computer-assisted audit tracks used by the Office of the Comptroller General of the Union to identify possible procurement irregularities, such as:

1. business relations between suppliers participating in the same procurement procedure
2. fractioning of contracts in order to use exemptions to the competitive procurement modality
3. non-compliance by suppliers with tender submission deadlines
4. registration of bid submissions on non-working days
5. supplier's bid submissions or company records with the same registered address
6. contract amounts above the legally prescribed ceiling for the procurement modality used
7. contract amendments within a month of contract award, in violation of the specific tender modality
8. evidence of bidder rotation in procurement procedures
9. use of reverse auctions for engineering services
10. micro- and small-sized enterprises with shareholders in other micro- and small-sized enterprises
11. personal relations between suppliers and public officials in procurement procedures
12. use of bid waiver when more than one "exclusive" supplier exists
13. bid submission received prior to publication of a procurement notice
14. possibility of competition in exemptions
15. participation of newly established suppliers in procurement procedures
16. contract amendments above an established limit, in violation of the specific tender modality
17. commitments issued prior to the original proposal date in the commitment registration system
18. bidding procedures involving suppliers registered in the Information Registry of Unpaid Federal Public Sector Credits (*CadastroInformativo de CréditosNãoQuitados do SetorPúblico Federal*)
19. micro- and small-sized enterprises linked to other enterprises
20. micro- and small-sized enterprises with earnings greater than BRL 0.24 million or BRL 2.40 million, respectively.

Source: OECD (forthcoming), *Compendium of Good Practices for Integrity in Public Procurement.*

Box 1.11. Transparency and traceability in public procurement in Italy

The Authority for the Supervision of Public Contracts has implemented a National Database on Public Contracts (NDPC) in line with Law n. 136/2010. It aims at collecting and processing data on public procurement in order to provide indications to the supervising departments and to inform regulators on measures that need to be taken to promote transparency, simplification and competition. It collects data on information technology and conducts market analyses. In particular, it collects and assesses data on:

- The structural characteristics of the public procurement market and its evolution. Statistics about the number and value of procurement awards are grouped by localisation, procurement entities, awarding procedures; the different typologies of procurement are periodically published.
- The criteria of efficiency and value for money during the procurement process. Modifications to contractual conditions are recorded in the authority's database which, in turn, detects dysfunctions and anomalies of the market.
- Dysfunctions and anomalies of the market through fixed measures. These dysfunctions and anomalies are detected through: *i)* the assessment indexes of excessive tendering rebates, with respect to the average rebates; *ii)* the number of bids to be presented in each awarding procedure; *iii)* the localisation of awarded companies with respect to the localisation of the contracting authority.

The Construction Company Database (*Casellario Informatico*) and the data on the declarations filed by the economic operators on the reliance on the capacities of other entities are, *inter alia*, parts of the National Database of Public Contracts.

Through the quality of the data made available by the NDPC, the authority improved its activities, notably supervision and regulation activity, in order to provide guidelines on measures that need to be taken into account to promote transparency, simplification and competition in the entire procurement process and, particularly, in the pre-bidding and post-bidding phases.

Source: OECD (2013b), *Colombia: Implementing Good Governance*, OECD Public Governance Reviews, OECD Publishing, Paris, http://dx.doi.org/10.1787/9789264202177-en.

The identification of potential cases of collusion or other anti-competitive behaviour is another area where improved access to reliable data can provide an initial warning system of cases that require deeper investigation. The Colombian *Superintendencia de Industria y Comercio* is developing such a system in Colombia, and integration with data from SECOP II could serve to improve the effectiveness and speed with which such a system operates. The *Superintendencia de Industria y Comercio* and CCE have developed a formal partnership to study procurement issues with competition implications following OECD recommendations and they should jointly develop training sessions and education activities to prevent and manage bid rigging to further implement such recommendations (OECD, 2014). This approach is being pursued in some OECD countries, for example Korea (see Box 1.12).

Box 1.12. **Korea's Bid Rigging Indicator Analysis System (BRIAS)**

The Fair Trade Commission (FTC) in Korea works with public buying entities to identify cartel activity and potential cases of bid rigging in public procurement. This work is particularly relevant at this time, as a number of potential cases related to increased spending in response to the 2009 economic crisis have been identified. During 2009 and 2010, Korea launched a number of large public works projects in a short period of time, and there are now claims that contractors colluded to divide this work.

To identify cases of collusion, the FTC traditionally relied on voluntary reporting by cartel members seeking leniency, and on reports by competing suppliers. These remain the most reliable sources of identification of potential collusion. In 2006, the FTC developed the Bid Rigging Indicator Analysis System (BRIAS) to supplement these methods of identification.

Drawing information directly from the Korean e-procurement system KONEPS, BRIAS looks to data elements including bidding price (as a ratio compared to reference price), the number of participants, and the competition method, and applies a formula that generates a potential bid-rigging score. If above a certain threshold, this then suggests the need to collect more information regarding the contract action. Based on this closer look, an investigation is opened in cases where it is warranted.

BRIAS collects information from KONEPS on a daily basis, and each month the system is run on collected data from the previous month. For goods and services, BRIAS is run on tenders above USD 423 800. For public works, the threshold is USD 4.2 million. As of 2012, BRIAS was run on 20 000-30 000 biddings per year; of approximately 20 000 runs in 2012, the system generated 200 hits that warranted an additional look. The establishment of this kind of automated system for the detection of red flags in public procurement is a good practice implemented successfully in other countries such as Brazil.

Whether identified through BRIAS or through traditional means, investigation of potential cases of collusion involves collection of additional information from PPS followed by site visitations and other investigative steps to find evidence of information exchange. These investigations can take anywhere from one to three years, from initial reporting to final verdict, and the FTC has established a separate investigation unit focused solely on public procurement. When found guilty, sanctions can range from orders for corrective action, which are essentially warnings for minor offenses, through a financial penalty of up to 10% of the contract volume involved. Additional criminal charges can also be filed with prosecutors. In 2012, more than 40 cases led to findings of guilt, leading to fines in excess of USD 847 million. The number of investigations and findings of guilt has been increasing.

In terms of direct contribution, the results from BRIAS have been limited: only three cases initially identified by BRIAS have led to findings of guilt. In part, this is attributable to the fact that the capacity to investigate is limited, and cases based on voluntary reporting or challenges by other suppliers begin with a more firm investigative basis than the circumstantial red flag generated by BRIAS. But during the period of its operation, voluntary reporting by cartel participants has increased significantly, and some of this increase is attributed to the raised awareness and fear of being caught generated by the implementation of the BRIAS system. This result is consistent with the OECD Recommendation on Public Procurement, which identifies the publication of risk management strategies, including systems for generating red flags, as an important element of their effectiveness.

To further expand the benefits of the BRIAS system, the FTC established a committee between project commissioners (including PPS and other large enterprises) to try to encourage adoption of a similar system at other public enterprises. In addition to providing the same functionality in a broader range of public procurement cases, spreading systems like this will allow the FTC to develop broader expertise, based on the differences in procurement practices at different entities, to better identify and prosecute cases of collusion. Dissemination activities are also undertaken to spread awareness and identify typical cases of collusion. In addition, the PPS training centre recently developed a separate training course on collusion, implemented in collaboration with the FTC.

Source: OECD (2016), *The Korean Public Procurement Service: Innovating for Effectiveness*, OECD Public Governance Reviews, OECD Publishing, Paris, http://dx.doi.org/10.1787/9789264249431-en.

Business intelligence and supplier utilisation

One of the recommendations from the 2013 procurement review of Colombia involved the development of business intelligence features to aggregate numbers, duration and amount of contract per product or service, as well as by buyer and supplier, to generate reports and statistical analysis to ensure proper visibility into public procurement spending. Many of these elements are envisioned in the reporting capabilities provided by SECOP II, but some countries are taking these efforts further into "supplier management" efforts. Designed to give the government more insight into the assets and capabilities of suppliers and their markets, such efforts represent a next step in effective utilisation of data to improve public procurement. One example is the management of supplier relationships in New Zealand (see Box 1.13).

Box 1.13. **Managing supplier relationships in collaborative contracts in New Zealand**

A New Zealand initiative to improve the performance of managing supplier relationships in collaborative contracts is applying a strategic supplier relationship management model.

All-of-government (AoG) contracts establish a single supply agreement between the Crown and approved suppliers for the supply of selected common goods and services purchased across government (see www.procurement.govt.nz). These contracts deliver a range of benefits to agencies, suppliers and, ultimately, the New Zealand taxpayer. These benefits include: cost-savings to agencies, the government and taxpayers; productivity gains for agencies and suppliers; and improved competition.

Strategic supplier relationship management (SSRM) is the systematic, enterprise-wide assessment of suppliers' assets and capabilities with respect to overall business strategy, determination of what activities to engage in with different suppliers, and planning and execution of all interactions with suppliers, in a co-ordinated fashion across the relationship lifecycle. The objective is to maximise the value realised through those interactions. The focus of SSRM is to develop two-way, mutually beneficial relationships with strategic supply partners to deliver greater levels of innovation and competitive advantage than could be achieved by operating independently or through a traditional, transactional purchasing arrangement.

Suppliers are encouraged to view SSRM in the AoG context as an attractive proposition as it helps them:

- better understand government's strategic direction to inform commercial strategies
- gain strategic alignment with New Zealand Government Procurement (NZGP) which can inform business planning
- better understand and inform category strategies
- gain early engagement with capability and capacity alignment
- discuss shared roadmaps and focused innovation opportunities
- receive strategic feedback from government on performance and identification of gaps that are effective their relationship with government
- better influence agency performance in contract utilisation and leverage.

Box 1.13. **Managing supplier relationships in collaborative contracts in New Zealand** *(continued)*

Key aspects of SSRM when applied to NZ common capability contracts include:

- A focus on procurement excellence across the plan, source, manage procurement lifecycle to maximise value for agencies.
- Assisting in maximising value during the contract management phase.
- Supplier classification enabling supplier focus and effort to be applied commensurate with the importance, value, risk and cost of the relationship.
- Models are applied to assist with classification, including Supply Positioning and Supply Preferencing.
- Providers are "classified" into one of three tiers:
  - Tier 3 = "light touch" – generally for the larger panels within professional services categories.
  - Tier 2 is similar to current effort across many of the current AOG contracts. It pertains mainly to majority of contracts within ICT and Corporate and Support Services.
  - Tier 1 provides for organisational alignment across three levels. It is more intense and is intended for the likes of key suppliers to government.

Source: Case study provided by New Zealand.

Recommendations

- CCE should develop metrics and continue to highlight the burden reduction associated with the move to electronic procurement processes, as a means of demonstrating value and attracting additional users.
- CCE should continue to carefully plan, monitor and evaluate the gradual implementation and expansion of SECOP II, applying appropriate change-management and communications strategies, to ensure the effectiveness of the new system. This could include connections with other systems, including subnational financial systems.
- CCE should continue implementation and expansion of standard reporting processes from the data available in SECOP II, including:
  - calculating on yearly basis the key performance indicators defined to monitor the health and function of the public procurement system and communicating them
  - reports designed to address specific stakeholder needs.
- CCE should consider the appropriate path forward to eliminate the duplication resulting from two mandatory supplier registry systems, the RUP and SECOP II.

- CCE should work with the Procuraduría and Contraloría to ensure that lessons learned from oversight activities are incorporated in policy development and training activities.
- CCE should consider additional opportunities to utilise SECOP II data in order to:
  - integrate with risk matrices used by the *Contraloría* in its activities
  - develop real-time risk management alerts
  - integrate with the anti-trust system for identifying collusion or cartel behaviour
  - develop supplier-focused business intelligence to better manage the procurement markets.

References

OECD (forthcoming), *Compendium of Good Practices for Integrity in Public Procurement.*

OECD (2016), *The Korean Public Procurement Service: Innovating for Effectiveness*, OECD Public Governance Reviews, OECD Publishing, Paris, http://dx.doi.org/10.1787/9789264249431-en.

OECD (2015a), "Recommendation of the Council on Public Procurement", www.oecd.org/corruption/recommendation-on-public-procurement.htm.

OECD (2015b), *Effective Delivery of Large Infrastructure Projects: The Case of the New International Airport of Mexico City*, OECD Public Governance Reviews, OECD Publishing, Paris, http://dx.doi.org/10.1787/9789264248335-en.

OECD (2015c), *Government at a Glance 2015*, OECD Publishing, Paris, http://dx.doi.org/10.1787/gov_glance-2015-en.

OECD (2014), "Fighting bid rigging in public procurement in Colombia: A secretariat report on Colombian procurement laws and practices", www.oecd.org/daf/competition/Booklet_SIC%20Procurement%20Report_16X23_REV_web.pdf.

OECD (2013a), *Implementing the OECD Principles for Integrity in Public Procurement: Progress since 2008*, OECD Public Governance Reviews, OECD Publishing, Paris, http://dx.doi.org/10.1787/9789264201385-en.

OECD (2013b), *Colombia: Implementing Good Governance*, OECD Public Governance Reviews, OECD Publishing, Paris, http://dx.doi.org/10.1787/9789264202177-en.

OECD (2013c), *Public Procurement Review of the State's Employees' Social Security and Social Services Institute in Mexico*, OECD Public Governance Reviews, OECD Publishing, Paris, http://dx.doi.org/10.1787/9789264197305-en.

Chapter 2

Improving Colombia's management of conflict of interest in public procurement

Public procurement is a complex activity involving multiple stakeholders at different stages, and this interaction between the public and the private sectors makes public procurement an area highly prone to corruption or integrity breaches. In particular, conflict of interest, generally used to describe the conflict between public official's public duty and his or her private interests, is a growing concern. Effective identification, prevention and management of conflicts of interest by an organisation are not only influenced by the controls and policies it implements, but also by its culture and prevention efforts. Active commitment and involvement from public servants are imperative to maintain an environment that stimulates integrity and rejects corruption and wrongdoing. In this light, this chapter describes the general context of Colombia's management of conflict of interest during the public procurement cycle and provides recommendations to improve it.

Public procurement, an activity prone to corruption

Corruption and integrity breaches are perceived to be common latent risks during the different phases of the public procurement cycle due to the financial interests at stake, the volume of transactions and the close interactions between the public and private sectors. Lack of transparency and weak governance systems particularly expose countries to these corruption risks. Unethical practices can occur in all phases of the public procurement and each phase has shown to be especially prone to different corruption risks, as shown in Table 2.1.

Table 2.1. **Corruption risks associated with the different phases of the procurement cycle**

Phase		Corruption risks
Risks of the pre-tendering phase	Needs assessment	• Lack of adequate needs assessment • Influence of external actors on officials decisions • Informal agreement on contract
	Planning and budgeting	• Poor procurement planning • Procurement not aligned with overall investment decision-making process • Failure to budget realistically or deficiency in the budget
	Development of specifications/ requirements	• Technical specifications are tailored for a specific company • Selection criteria is not objectively defined and no established in advance • Requesting samples of goods and services that can influence • Buying information on the project specifications.
Risks of the tendering phase	Choice of procurement procedure	• Lack of procurement integrity for the use of non-competitive procedures • Abuse of non-competitive procedures on the basis of legal exceptions: contract splitting, abuse of extreme urgency, non-supported modifications
	Request for proposal/bid	• Absence of public notice for the invitation to bid • Evaluation and award criteria are not announced • Procurement information is disclose and made public
	Bid submission	• Lack of competition or cases of collusive bidding: o cover bidding o bid suppression o bid rotation o market allocation
	Bid evaluation	• Conflict of interest and corruption in the evaluation process through: o familiarity with bidders over time o personal interests such as gifts or future/additional employment o no effective implementation of the "four eyes-principle"
	Contract award	• Vendors fail to disclose accurate cost or pricing data in their price proposals, resulting in an increased contract price (i.e. invoice mark-ups, channel stuffing) • Conflict of interest and corruption in the approval process (i.e. no effective separation of financial, contractual and project authorities) • Lack access to records on the procedure
+ Risks of the post-award phase	Contract management/ performance	• Abuses of the supplier in performing the contract, in particular in relation to its quality, price and timing: • Substantial change in contract conditions to allow more time and/ or higher prices for the bidder • Product substitution or sub-standard work or service not meeting contract specifications • Theft of new assets before delivery to end-user or before being recorded • Deficient supervision from public officials and/or collusion between contractors and supervising officials • Subcontractors and partners chosen in an on-transparent way or not kept accountable
	Order and payment	• Deficient separation of financial duties and/or lack of supervision of public officials leading to: • False accounting and cost misallocation or cost migration between contracts • Late payments of invoices • False or duplicate invoicing for good and services not supplied and for interim payment in advance entitlement

Source: Adapted from OECD (2007), *Integrity in Public Procurement: Good Practice from A to Z*, OECD Publishing, Paris, http://dx.doi.org/10.1787/9789264027510-en.

The close relation between these integrity risks requires a holistic and integrated approach to properly address the issue, involving both public and private actors at different phases of the procurement cycle. If not adequately managed, such integrity risks during the procurement process pose a great threat to sound economic performance and effective governance of public functions.

Corruption, wrongdoing and integrity breaches can have a profound impact on Colombia's capacity to maximise the use of available resources to provide the volume of high quality services required by its citizens. As mentioned, one of these risks is the presence of conflicts of interest that may affect the objectivity of a public official's decisions. As such, it is essential that Colombia takes concrete and strong actions to identify, manage and prevent conflicts of interest in its procurement activities and to implement appropriate remedial actions, thereby increasing the integrity of its procurement function.

Enhancing the policy framework to address conflicts of interest

Providing a clear definition of conflict of interest is essential for a coherent and consistent approach

Serving the public interest is the fundamental mission of governments and public institutions. Thus governments and public institutions are obligated to ensure that public officials do not allow their private interests and affiliations to compromise official decision making and public management. Especially in times of an increasingly demanding society, inadequately identified and managed conflicts of interest on the part of public officials, which can result in corruption, could compromise citizens' trust in public institutions. Therefore, a coherent and consistent policy framework for an adequate management of conflict of interest needs to be built.

The framework needs to rely on a clear definition of conflict of interest to enable an objective and effective identification and management of conflict-of-interest situations. The OECD provides the following definition: a "conflict of interest" involves a conflict between the public duty and private interests of a public official, in which the public official has private-capacity interests that could improperly influence the performance of his/her official duties and responsibilities. In layman's terms, it is a situation in which a public official has a private or other interest which is such as to influence, or appear to influence, the impartial and objective performance of his or her official duties (Reed, 2008).

The "OECD Guidelines for Managing Conflict of Interest in the Public Service" also distinguish between *actual*, *apparent* and *potential* conflict-of-interest situations. Actual conflict of interest is a direct conflict between a public official's current duties and responsibilities and his or her private interests, whereas apparent conflict of interest occurs when a public official's private interests could improperly influence the performance of his/her duties, but this is not, in fact, the case. Furthermore, potential conflict of interest involves a situation in which a public official has private interests which are such that a conflict of interest would arise if the official were to become involved in the relevant official responsibilities in the future.

Implementing appropriate measures for apparent and potential conflicts-of-interest situations are as important as preventing and managing actual conflict-of-interest situations. Along with the rapidly changing public sector environment, new forms of conflict of interest emerge involving an individual official's private interests and public duties. In this sense, it is crucial to have a clear legal framework for public procurement agents' activities against any actual, apparent and potential conflicts of interest so that their decisions cannot be influenced by personal preferences or those of family, friends or past or future associates.

Countries have implemented different approaches that reflect their country environments, including political systems and culture. The two major approaches can be found in the OECD countries. They define conflict of interest either descriptively or prescriptively.

The descriptive approach defines conflict-of-interest situations in general terms and provides public officials with the general features of the phenomenon. General principles together with exemplified general cases provide guidance for public officials in preventing and avoiding conflict-of-interest situations. In this approach general principles play the primary role by stating what is expected of public officials in general, while specific rules and procedures have a complementary role.

The prescriptive approach defines a range of specific situations that are considered incompatible with public office or in conflict with the public interest and official duties. This rules-based approach provides public officials with detailed enforceable standards, generally in legal regulations. However, these standards are ultimately based on fundamental public service principles that can also embody aspirational goals (Box 2.1).

Box 2.1. **The difference between a principles versus rules-based approach to managing conflicts of interest**

	Principles-based approach, e.g. United Kingdom	Rules-based approach, e.g. United States[1]
Responsibility	Dispersed across government	Office of Government Ethics
Authority	No specific conflict of interest legislation. Local guidance. Companies Act applies to directors. Management code specifies some "rules".	Enforceable conflict of interest prohibitions defined in statute with criminal or civil penalties.
Other standards	Behavioural and ethical standards defined in codes of conduct and "Nolan principles".	Civil restrictions for certain outside activities. Administrative standards of conduct.
Disclosure requirements	Devolved, voluntary disclosure system for civil servants. MPs' financial interests are declared and published. Information on Senior civil servants and ministerial hospitality, gifts, travel and external meetings is published.	Central mandatory financial disclosure systems: • Public reporting is required for all senior officials. • Other employees make confidential financial disclosures.

1. US Office of Government Ethics, www.oge.gov/Topics/Financial-Conflicts-of-Interest-and-Impartiality/Financial-Conflicts-of-Interest---Impartiality/ and Ley, J. S., "Managing conflicts of interest in the executive branch: The experience of the United States", in OECD (2004), *Managing Conflict of Interest in the Public Service: OECD Guidelines and Country Experiences*, OECD Publishing, Paris, http://dx.doi.org/10.1787/9789264104938-en, pp. 231-249.

Source: National Audit Office (2015), "Conflicts of interest", Report by the Comptroller and Auditor General, Session 2014-15, 27 January, www.nao.org.uk/wp-content/uploads/2015/01/Conflicts-of-interest.pdf (accessed 28 January 2016).

In Colombia, the provisions in regulations and laws list the circumstances and relationships that could lead to a conflict of interest, and thus those that public servants are prohibited from.[1] These specific prohibitions and disqualifications include, among others, parties that have financed the political campaigns of presidents, governors or mayors; former public servants in matters related with their former position; and parties having relationship with the public servants in directive positions within the procuring government agency. According to the aforementioned distinction, Colombia takes a prescriptive approach in addressing conflicts of interest, making reference to: *i)* situations affecting the legal capacity of the contractor and/or the public officials to enter into a contract; and *ii)* special relationships between parties interested in a selection process and public officials affecting the equal treatment. The fact that such potential or apparent conflict-of-interest situations or events are not listed in one regulation makes detection and enforcement difficult. In addition, the prescriptive approach impedes swift action in cases that are not listed yet where the conflict between the public and private interest is evident.

Regardless of the approach a country takes, a clear definition of conflict of interest should be a premise. Without a clear definition of conflict of interest in its legislation, this approach could suffer from incompleteness and inflexibility, especially when new conflicts-of-interest situations arise. Colombia could clearly define conflict of interest in its legislation, especially in its procurement legislation, as found in OECD countries such as Canada and New Zealand (Box 2.2).

Increasing complexity of public sector requires tailored conflict-of-interest policy for public procurement officials

Many governments are experiencing increasing interaction between the public and private sectors and new forms of relationships have been developed between the public sector, businesses and non-profit sector. As all public officials have legitimate interests which arise out of their capacity as private citizens, conflicts of interest cannot simply be avoided or prohibited by imposing restrictions on conflict-of-interest situations that have been observed to date, and must be adequately and appropriately defined, identified and managed.

Recognising the risks associated with specific public functions, increasing number of OECD countries are implementing tailored policy and rules to address them (Figure 2.1). Furthermore, almost 50% of OECD countries have developed specific conflict-of-interest policies for procurement officials to respond to the red flags raised by public procurement as a major interface between the public and private sectors. Despite the relevance of this issue, Colombia has not yet developed specific policy or rules for any particular category of public officials, including for public procurement officials.

Colombia could develop a specific conflict-of-interest policy for procurement officials. This tailored policy for public procurement should include the relationships and situations that are most relevant to the Colombian context to be an effective measure to prevent and manage conflict of interest of public procurement officials, as seen, for instance, in Mexico and the United Kingdom (Box 2.3).

Box 2.2. **Definition of conflict of interest adopted by OECD member countries**

Canada

Canada's Conflict of Interest Act (S.C. 2006, c.9, s.2) states "a public office holder is in a conflict of interest when he or she exercises an official power, duty or function that provides an opportunity to further his or her private interests or those of his or her relatives or friends or to improperly further another person's private interests" (Article 4). Furthermore, the Act also specifies the general duty expected of public servants in Article 5 – "Every public office holder shall arrange his or her private affairs in a manner that will prevent the public office holder from being in a conflict of interest." While the Conflict of Interest Act is primarily aimed at elected and other senior officials, the Treasury Board Code of Values and Ethics applies this definition and similar responsibilities to every public servant in government.

New Zealand

In New Zealand, the definition of conflict of interest is tailored to targeted groups, such as public servants, ministers or board members of crown companies. Nevertheless, these definitions contain common features. For example, they all cover actual and perceived as well as direct and indirect conflicts. In addition to the general definitions developed for the targeted groups outlined here, supplementing documents also list possible types of conflict-of-interest situations, together with concrete practical examples.

For public servants: "Conflicts of interest are defined as, … any financial or other interest or undertaking that could directly or indirectly compromise the performance of their duties, or the standing of their department in its relationships with the public, clients, or ministers. This would include any situation where actions taken in an official capacity could be seen to influence or be influenced by an individual's private interests (e.g. company directorships, shareholdings, offers of outside employment). […] A potential area of conflict exists for public servants who may have to deal directly with members of Parliament who have approached the department in a private capacity" (Code of Conduct).

For ministers: "Conflicts of interest can arise because of the influence and power they wield – both in the individual performance of their portfolio responsibilities and as members of Cabinet. Ministers must conduct themselves at all times in the knowledge that their role is a public one; appearances and propriety can be as important as actual conflict of interest in establishing what is acceptable behaviour. A conflict of interest may be pecuniary (that is, arising from the Minister's direct financial interests) or non-pecuniary (concerning, for example, a member of the Minister's family) that may be either direct or indirect" (Cabinet Manual).

For board members of Crown companies, a conflict of interest is defined as a situation in which a board member is "party to, or will or may derive a material financial benefit from" a transaction involving his or her company (The Companies Act 1993, Part VIII, Sections 138 and 139).

Sources: Treasury Board Code of Values and Ethics (2006), "Conflict of Interest Act", Canada, www.tbs-sct.gc.ca/pol/index-eng.aspx?|=V; OECD (2004), *Managing Conflict of Interest in the Public Service: OECD Guidelines and Country Experiences*, OECD Publishing, Paris, http://dx.doi.org/10.1787/9789264104938-en.

Figure 2.1. **Development of specific conflict-of-interest policy/rules for particular categories of public officials in OECD 32**

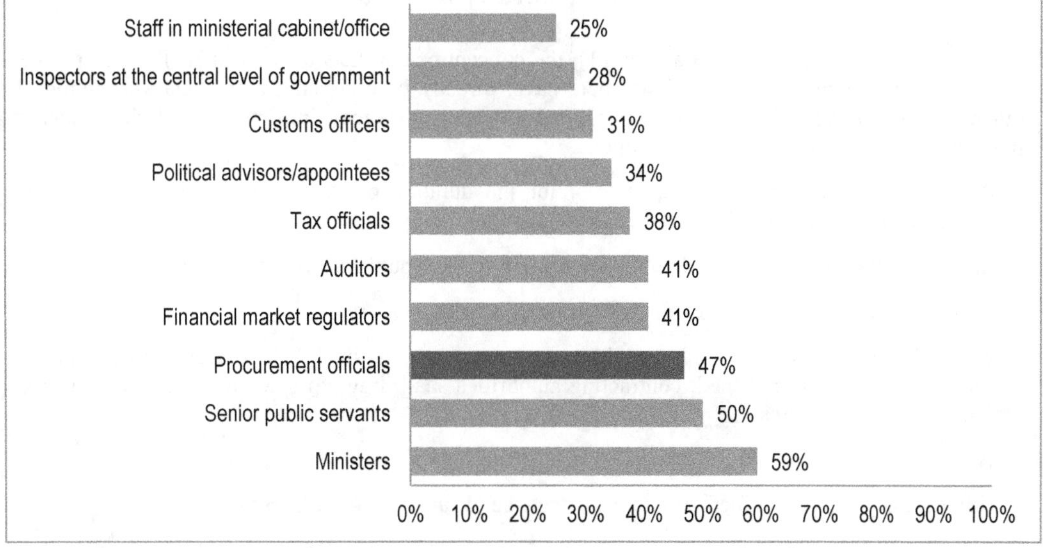

Category	%
Staff in ministerial cabinet/office	25%
Inspectors at the central level of government	28%
Customs officers	31%
Political advisors/appointees	34%
Tax officials	38%
Auditors	41%
Financial market regulators	41%
Procurement officials	47%
Senior public servants	50%
Ministers	59%

0% 10% 20% 30% 40% 50% 60% 70% 80% 90% 100%

Source: OECD (2014), "Survey on Managing Conflict of Interest in the Executive Branch and Whistleblower Protection".

Box 2.3. **Conflict-of-interest policies for public procurement officials in OECD member countries**

Mexico

In early 2015, the President of Mexico issued a series of Executive Orders to strengthen public sector integrity focused primarily on preventing and managing conflict of interest, including the disclosure of potential conflict of interest of the public servant and his/her family member in their yearly asset declaration. The Executive Orders also require the issuances of a Code of Ethics for all public servants of the Federal Government and guidance for public procurement officials when interacting with suppliers (*Protocolo de actuación de los servidores públicos en contrataciones públicas*); the creation of a classification and registry for procurement officials, the certification of procurement officials, the online publication of sanctioned suppliers; increased collaboration with chambers of commerce; an online "one-stop shop" (*ventanilla única*) for transactions with government to reduce potential opportunities for bribery; and the creation of a Special Unit on Ethics and Conflict of Interests Prevention (*Unidad Especializada en Ética y Prevención de Conflictos de Interés*).

United Kingdom

The Public Contracts Regulations 2015

24. (1) Contracting authorities shall take appropriate measures to effectively prevent, identify and remedy conflicts of interest arising in the conduct of procurement procedures so as to avoid any distortion of competition and to ensure equal treatment of all economic operators.

Box 2.3. **Conflict-of-interest policies for public procurement officials in OECD member countries** *(continued)*

(2) For the purposes of paragraph (1), the concept of conflicts of interest shall at least cover any situations where relevant staff members have, directly or indirectly, a financial, economic or other personal interest which might be perceived to compromise their impartiality and independence in the context of the procurement procedure.

83. Contracting authorities shall, at least for the duration of the contract, keep copies of all concluded contracts with a value equal to or greater than:

(a) EUR 1 million in the case of public supply contracts or public service contracts

(b) EUR 10 million in the case of public works contracts.

84. (1) For every contract or framework agreement covered by this Part, and every time a dynamic purchasing system is established, contracting authorities shall draw up a written report which shall include at least the following:

[...]

(i) where applicable, conflicts of interest detected and subsequent measures taken.

Sources: OECD (2015a), *Effective Delivery of Large Infrastructure Projects: The Case of the New International Airport of Mexico City*, OECD Public Governance Reviews, OECD Publishing, Paris, http://dx.doi.org/10.1787/9789264248335-en; UK Government (2015), "The Public Contracts Regulations 2015", www.legislation.gov.uk/uksi/2015/102/pdfs/uksi_20150102_en.pdf.

Raising awareness through developing and disseminating a dedicated code of conduct

Standards of conduct are recognised as essential for guiding the behaviour of public officials in line with the public purpose of the organisation in which they work. The "OECD Principles for Improving Ethical Conduct in the Public Service" acknowledge the critical role of, and provide guidance to decision makers and public managers on high standards of conduct for a cleaner public administration. Thanks to their concise focus, flexible nature and straightforward language, codes of conduct have proven to be instrumental in promoting integrity in any organisation as they provide a clear benchmark for acceptable behaviour and ethical standards against which personnel and the institution itself can be held accountable. A code of conduct can be seen as a sort of contract among employees within the organisation, as well as a statement to third parties about the ethical standards to expect and respect (CCAB, 2014) (Box 2.4).

Box 2.4. **The impact of codes of ethics: Research and empirical findings**

Research in public administration into ethics codes has been very limited. In his surveys among members of the American Society for Public Administration (Bowman and Williams, 1997; Bowman, 1990), Bowman found that practitioners tend to think positively about codes and to believe that they have desirable effects. Flake and Grob (1998) performed content analyses on public sector ethics codes and found that they were "dramatically skewed in the low-road direction", i.e. they emphasised compliance with rules and laws. These and other analyses are interesting, but "a relationship between codes and actual behaviour in fact still awaits examination" (Gilman and Lewis, 1996) . One public administration study (among city and county managers) into the topic found "no significant difference in the mean response scores [on a moral reasoning test] that can be attributed to whether or not a jurisdiction has a code of ethics" (Stewart and Sprinthall, 1993).

An interesting descriptive study is the 2007 Survey of the New Zealand State Services Commission, which was conducted by the Ethics Resource Centre among 4 642 State servants. Some 96% of the responding state servants reported that their agency had drafted standards of integrity and conduct. Half of surveyed state servants reported that their agency had a specific person, telephone line, e-mail address, or website where they could get advice about integrity and conduct issues. In sum, the findings were very mixed. This is consistent with the hypothesis that an integrity code will only have a significant impact when it is embedded in and consistent with a wider integrity management framework.

Source: OECD (2013a), *OECD Integrity Review of Italy: Reinforcing Public Sector Integrity, Restoring Trust for Sustainable Growth*, OECD Public Governance Reviews, OECD Publishing, Paris, http://dx.doi.org/10.1787/9789264193819-en.

In addition to code of conduct, guidelines could further complement the policy framework for identifying and managing conflicts of interest. The main roles of such guidelines are providing specific conflict-of-interest situations focused on public procurement activities and a range of practical examples of concrete steps to be taken in order to resolve such situations. The complementing documents regarding conflicts-of-interest regulations should not only remind the public procurement officials what is expected of them in cases of any actual, apparent and potential conflicts-of-interest situations, but also promote the values that they are expected to pursue as an individual public servant as well as a public administration body. They could further benefit the public procurement system from being further extended to all the stakeholders involved in the public procurement, not only for the public procurement officials but also the contractors, suppliers, consultants, auditors, etc. Colombia could develop a code of conduct for procurement officials as well as for those involved in the procurement process, including suppliers, bidders, subcontractors and temporary staff, not covered by public officials rules (see Box 2.5 as an example from Canada).

Box 2.5. **Code of conduct for procurement in Canada**

The Government of Canada is responsible for maintaining the confidence of the vendor community and the Canadian public in the procurement system, by conducting procurement in an accountable, ethical and transparent manner.

The Code of Conduct for Procurement will aid the Government in fulfilling its commitment to reform procurement, ensuring greater transparency, accountability, and the highest standards of ethical conduct. The Code consolidates the Government's existing legal, regulatory and policy requirements into a concise and transparent statement of the expectations the Government has of its employees and its suppliers.

The Code of Conduct for Procurement provides all those involved in the procurement process – public servants and vendors alike – with a clear statement of mutual expectations to ensure a common basic understanding among all participants in procurement.

The Code reflects the policy of the Government of Canada and is framed by the principles set out in the Financial Administration Act and the Federal Accountability Act. It consolidates the Federal Government's measures on conflict of interest, post-employment measures and anti-corruption as well as other legislative and policy requirements relating specifically to procurement. This Code is intended to summarise existing law by providing a single point of reference to key responsibilities and obligations for both public servants and vendors. In addition, it describes vendor complaints and procedural safeguards.

The Government expects that all those involved in the procurement process will abide by the provisions of this Code.

Source: *Public Works and Government Services Canada* (PWGSC) (n.d.), *"The Code of Conduct for Procurement"*, www.tpsgc-pwgsc.gc.ca/app-acq/cndt-cndct/contexte-context-eng.html (accessed 17 June 2015).

Colombia could also develop practical guidelines and scenarios on conflict of interest to help public officials identify and manage such situations, as done by the Government of Western Australia (Box 2.6).

Box 2.6. **Conflict of interest guidelines of the Government of Western Australia**

The Integrity Coordinating Group (ICG) of the Government of Western Australia has developed guidelines to help public officers identify and manage conflicts of interest.

The guidelines provide public authorities with information and practical tools about integrity in decision making, which can be used to strengthen and sustain their decision-making processes. The following questions are addressed:

- What is a conflict of interest?
- Is it wrong to have a conflict of interest?
- Who is responsible for identifying and managing conflicts of interest?
- How can officers identify if a conflict of interest exists?

Box 2.6. **Conflict of interest guidelines of the Government of Western Australia** *(continued)*

To identify conflict of interest, the ICG suggests considering the "6Ps".

Public duty versus private interests	Do I have personal or private interests that may conflict, or be perceived to conflict with my public duty?
Potentialities	Could there be benefits for me now, or in the future, that could cast doubt on my objectivity?
Perception	Remember, perception is important. How will my involvement in the decision/action be viewed by others?
Proportionality	Does my involvement in the decision appear fair and reasonable in all the circumstances?
Presence of mind	What are the consequences if I ignore a conflict of interest? What if my involvement was questioned publicly?
Promises	Have I made any promises or commitments in relation to the matter? Do I stand to gain or lose from the proposed action/decision?

The ICG has also provided major options, or "6Rs", for officers and supervisors to manage conflicts of interest.

Record/register	Recording the disclosure of a conflict of interest in a register is an important first step; however, this does not necessarily resolve the conflict. It may be necessary to assess the situation and determine whether one or more of the following strategies is also required.
Restrict	It may be appropriate to restrict your involvement in the matter, for example, refrain from taking part in debate about a specific issue, abstain from voting on decisions, and/ or restrict access to information relating to the conflict of interest. If this situation occurs frequently, and an ongoing conflict of interest is likely, other options may need to be considered.
Recruit	If it is not practical to restrict your involvement, an independent third party may need to be engaged to participate in, oversee, or review the integrity of the decision-making process.
Remove	Removal from involvement in the matter altogether is the best option when ad hoc or recruitment strategies are not feasible, or appropriate.
Relinquish	Relinquishing the personal or private interests may be a valid strategy for ensuring there is no conflict with your public duty. This may be the relinquishment of shares, or membership of a club or association.
Resign	Resignation may be an option if the conflict of interest cannot be resolved in any other way, particularly where conflicting private interests cannot be relinquished.

The ICG recognises there cannot be a "one-size-fits-all" approach to conflicts of interest across the public sector. These scenarios are designed to provide practical tips for identifying and managing some of the more common conflict-of-interest situations:

- sponsorship from the private sector
- wearing two hats – dual roles as a public officer
- representative members on boards and committees
- allocation of grants for community-based services
- gifts, benefits and hospitality
- recruitment, selection and appointment
- secondary employment
- managing procurement processes, tenders and contracts.

The scenarios illustrate examples of how conflicts of interest may be identified and what strategies may be employed to manage them. The choice of strategies may vary across the sector, and will depend on the operating environment, legislative requirements and practical solutions.

Sources: Integrity Coordinating Group (2011), *"Conflicts of Interests Guidelines for the Western Australia Public Sector"*, https://icg.wa.gov.au/sites/default/files/documents/Conflicts%20of%20interest%20-%20Guidelines%20for%20the%20WA%20public%20sector.pdf; Integrity Coordinating Group (n.d.), *"Conflicts of interest - guidelines and scenarios"*, https://icg.wa.gov.au/node/81.

Training programmes and guidance are effective communicational tools

Adopting a code of conduct or guidelines have a communicational aspect as it sends a strong signal that the organisation is committed to observing the highest standards of integrity and that ethical behaviour is expected from all employees (Transparency International, 2014). Yet, a code of conduct alone would not suffice if it is not complemented by appropriate organisational strategy, managerial guidance and support and training programmes. Ethics or integrity training for procurement officials can raise awareness and develop knowledge of, and commitment to, the critical elements of a culture of integrity in public organisations.

Ethical training displays high importance since it provides practical guidance on ethical behaviour in situations where official rules contradict traditions or do not provide clear answers on how to behave in concrete situations. It is especially important in countries with high levels of corruption where many grey areas have not yet been addressed by formal rules. While lectures appear appropriate for training on rules, interactive and tailor-made practical methods may be more useful for training on values and ethical conduct in risk situations (OECD, 2013b).

In Colombia, trainings are provided within the broader context of procurement system training offered by the Inspector General of Colombia (*Procuraduría General de la Nación*), on an irregular basis. Colombia could greatly benefit from providing dedicated and systematic ethics or integrity trainings that are offered on a regular basis, and eventually extending the training to more stakeholders, including suppliers and contractors (see Boxes 2.7 and 2.8 for examples from Germany and France on specialised trainings).

Box 2.7. **Integrity training in Germany**

The Federal Procurement Agency is a government agency which manages purchasing for 26 different federal authorities, foundations and research institutions that fall under the responsibility of the Federal Ministry of the Interior. It is the second largest federal procurement agency after the Federal Office for Defence Technology and Procurement.

The Procurement Agency has taken several measures to promote integrity among its personnel, including support and advice by a corruption prevention officer ("Contact Person for the Prevention of Corruption"), the organisation of workshops and training on corruption and the rotation of its employees.

Since 2001, it is mandatory for new staff members to participate in a corruption-prevention workshop. They learn about the risks of getting involved in bribery and the briber's possible strategies. They also learn how to behave when these situations occur; for example, they are encouraged to report it ("blow the whistle"). Workshops highlight the central role of employees whose ethical behaviour is an essential part of corruption prevention. About ten workshops took place with 190 persons who provided positive feedback concerning the content and the usefulness of the training. The involvement of the Agency's "Contact Person for the Prevention of Corruption" and the Head of the Department for Central Services in the workshops demonstrated to participants that corruption prevention is one of the priorities for the agency. In 2005 the target group of the workshops was enlarged to include not only induction training but also ongoing training for the entire personnel. Since then, six to seven workshops are being held per year at regular intervals, training approximately 70 new and existing employees per year.

Another key corruption prevention measure is the staff rotation after a period of five to eight years in order to avoid prolonged contact with suppliers, as well as improve motivation and make the job more attractive. However, the rotation of members of staff still meets with difficulty in the Agency. Due to a high level of specialisation, many officials cannot change their organisational unit, their knowledge being indispensable for the work of the unit. In these cases alternative measures such as intensified (supervisory) control are being taken.

Source: Federal Procurement Agency, Germany.

Box 2.8. Specialised training for public procurement in France

The Central Service of Corruption Prevention, an inter-ministerial body attached to the Ministry of Justice in France has developed training material for public procurement to help officials identify irregularities and corruption in procurement. Below is a case study excerpted from the training material, which illustrates the challenges faced by various actors at different steps of the procedure. It also highlights the difficulty of gathering evidence on irregularities and corruption.

Issue at stake

Following an open invitation to bid, an unsuccessful bidder complains to the mayor of a commune accusing the bidding panel of irregularities because his bid was lower than that submitted by the winning bidder. How should the mayor deal with the problem?

Stage 1: Checking compliance with public procurement procedures

The firm making the complaint is well known and is not considered "litigious". The mayor therefore gives its claim his attention and requests that the internal audit service check the conditions of the award of contract, particularly whether the procedure was in compliance with the regulations (the lowest bidder is not necessarily the best bidder) and with the notices published in the official journal. The mayor learns from the report prepared by the bidding committee that although the procedure was in accordance with the regulations, the bid by the firm in question had been revised upwards by the technical service responsible for comparing the offers. Apparently the firm had omitted certain cost headings which were added on to its initial bid.

Stage 2: Replying to the losing bidder

The mayor lets the losing bidder know exactly why its bid was unsuccessful. However, by return post, he receives a letter pointing out that no one had informed the company of the change made to its bid, which was in fact unjustified since the expenditure that had purportedly been omitted had in fact been included in the bid under another heading.

Stage 3: Suspicions

The internal audit service confirms the unsuccessful bidder's claim and points out that nothing in the report helps to establish any grounds for the change made by the technical service. It also points out that it would be difficult for an official with any experience, however little, not to see that the expenses had been accounted for under another heading. The mayor now requests the audit service to find out whether the technical service is in the habit of making such changes, whether it has already processed bids from the winning bidder and if contracts were frequently awarded to the latter. He also requests that it check out the background of the officials concerned by the audit. Do they have experience? Have they been trained? Do they have links with the successful contractor?

Could they have had links with them in their previous posts? What do their wives and children do? Examination of the personnel files of the officials and the shares of the company which won the contract fail to find anything conclusive: the only links between the officials or their families and the successful bidder are indirect.

Stage 4: Handing the case over to authorities of the Ministry of Justice

Having suspicions, but no proof, the mayor hands over information so that investigations can begin. The investigators now have to find proof that a criminal offence (favouritism, corruption, undue advantage, etc.) has been committed and will exercise their powers to examine bank accounts, conduct hearings, surveillance, etc. The case has now moved out of the domain of public procurement regulations and into the domain of criminal proceedings.

Conclusion

Unable to gather any evidence and with no authority to conduct an in-depth investigation or question the parties concerned, the mayor makes the only decision that is within his power, which is to reorganise internally and change the duties of the two members of staff concerned. However, he must proceed cautiously when giving the reasons for his decision so as to avoid exposing innocent people to public condemnation or himself to accusations of defamation while the criminal investigation is in progress.

The mayor also decides that from then on the report by the technical services to the bidding committee should give a fuller explanation of its calculations and any changes it makes to the bids, as well as systematically inform bidders of any changes.

Source: OECD (2007), *Integrity in Public Procurement: Good Practice from A to Z*, OECD Publishing, Paris, http://dx.doi.org/10.1787/9789264027510-en.

A balanced management approach is key for sound implementation

A strict approach to manage conflicts of interest could damage efficiency in public procurement

Colombia specifies prohibitions on relationships from which conflicts of interest may arise or materialise in the relevant laws and regulations. Additionally, all the sanctions imposed by government agencies regarding procurement activities are recorded on the suppliers' registry.

During the selection process, each procurement agency is obliged to review the Unique Proponents Registry (RUP, or *Registro Único de Proponentes)* to verify that the public procurement officials and bidders are not subject to any specific prohibitions and disqualifications mentioned in the relevant provisions of regulations and to review the existence of any disciplinary or fiscal decisions on the websites of the Inspector General Office and the General Comptroller Office.

According to the interviews with the public procurement officials during the fact-finding mission, public procurement officials are more concerned with the sanctions in cases of breach in conflicts-of-interest regulations than the private sector actors. In consequence, this could result in excessive application of preclusion of potential bidders, thus limiting the potential economic benefits that could come from increasing competition in the public procurement process. At the same time, preclusion does not mean resolution of conflicts of interest, thus requiring a balanced management approach to uphold integrity through adequately identifying, preventing, and managing conflicts of interest in the public service. In this regard, *Colombia Compra Eficiente* could consider implementing additional declaration and evaluation steps prior to preclusion of the bidders from the process, as seen in Australia (Box 2.9).

Box 2.9. **Conflict-of-interest management during tender evaluation in Australia**

The Government of South Australia's Department of Planning, Transport and Infrastructure (DPTI) suggests ways to address potential and material conflict-of-interest situations during the procurement process through the Procurement Management Framework. It states that the DPTI staff member should notify the evaluation Panel Chairperson as soon as they notice any apparent conflict-of-interest situation. Even though a potential conflict of interest will not necessarily preclude a person from being involved in the evaluation process, it is declared and can be independently assessed.

It also lists situations that would be considered as a material conflict of interest of a staff in relation to a company submitting a tender including: *i)* a significant shareholding in a small private company which is submitting a tender; *ii)* having an immediate relative (e.g. son, daughter, partner, sibling) employed by a company which is tendering, even though that person is not involved in the preparation of the tender and winning the tender would have a material impact on the company; *iii)* having a relative who is involved in the preparation of the tender to be submitted by a company; *iv)* exhibiting a bias or partiality for or against a tender (e.g. because of events that occurred during a previous contract); *v)* a person, engaged under a contract to assist DPTI with the assessment, assessing a direct competitor who is submitting a tender; *vi)* regularly socialising with an employee of tenderer who is involved with the preparation of the tender; *vii)* having received gifts, hospitality or similar benefits from a tenderer in the period leading up to the call of tenders; *viii)* having recently left the employment of a tenderer; or *ix)* considering an offer of future employment or some other inducement from a tenderer.

Source: Department of Planning, Transport and Infrastructure (DPTI) (n.d.), "Procurement Management Framework: Confidentiality and Conflict of Interest", PR115, http://dpti.sa.gov.au/__data/assets/pdf_file/0015/114351/PR115Confidentiality_and_Conflict_of_Interest.pdf (accessed 16 June 2015).

In addition, implementing a positive management strategy to complement Colombia's prescriptive legal approach could further enhance the framework for identifying and managing conflict of interest by promoting values and ethics among public procurement officials. The "OECD Guidelines for Managing Conflict of Interest in the Public Service" provide for policy options for positive resolution or management of a continuing or pervasive conflict (Box 2.10). In fact, many OECD countries are using several of the following options according to the situations and the seniority or decision-making power of the public officials. Colombia could consider including in their approach options for positive resolution or management of conflict of interest for public procurement officials.

Box 2.10. **OECD Guidelines for Managing Conflict of Interest in the Public Service**

The "OECD Guidelines for Managing Conflict of Interest in the Public Sector" set the international benchmark to help governments review and develop comprehensive conflict-of-interest policies for the public sector.

The guidelines state the importance of setting clear rules on what is expected of public officials in dealing with conflict-of-interest situations in order to provide a coherent and consistent approach to managing conflict-of-interest situations. They also list options for positive resolution or management of a continuing or pervasive conflict which could include one or more of several strategies as appropriate, for example:

- divestment or liquidation of the interest by the public official
- recusal of the public official from involvement in an affected decision-making process
- restriction of access by the affected public official to particular information
- transfer of the public official to duty in a non-conflicting function
- re-arrangement of the public official's duties and responsibilities
- assigning of the conflicting interest in a genuinely "blind trust" arrangement
- resignation of the public official from the conflicting private-capacity function
- resignation of the public official from his/her public office.

Source: OECD (2004), *Managing Conflict of Interest in the Public Service: OECD Guidelines and Country Experiences*, OECD Publishing, Paris, http://dx.doi.org/10.1787/9789264104938-en.

Proactive management of conflicts of interest through private interest disclosure

Disclosure of private interests by public officials and making them public is an effective tool for managing conflict of interest. On the one hand, it holds public officials more accountable of their actions by making their private interests more transparent. On the other hand, it could raise concern over potential harming of the public officials' privacy. Accordingly, countries should direct efforts to strike the right balance; increasing numbers of OECD countries apply more extensive disclosure requirements according to the seniority of the public officials or the nature of the positions concerned.

In the context of Colombia, public officials are required to register in the *Sistema de Información y Gestión del Empleo Público* (SIGEP), operated by *Función Pública.* Registration includes a statement of assets and income, as well as information on private economic activities. SIGEP registry is a condition precedent to beginning service as a public official, and must be updated annually and at the end of the term of public service. The head of human resources at each government agency verifies the data registered in SIGEP, but only the previous employment of public officials are disclosed and made publicly available. Furthermore, the same level of disclosure and public availability of private interests apply to all public officials, regardless of the seniority or the position; the public officials in "at-risk" areas, e.g. public procurement officials, tax and customs officials and financial authorities, also have the same requirements. In this regard, Colombia could benefit from implementing a more tailored approach to disclosure and public availability requirements concerning the public officials' private interests who are exposed to more risks of conflict of interest, an in particular, procurement officials (see Figure 2.2 and Box 2.11).

Figure 2.2. **Level of disclosure and public availability of private interests by the level of public officials in the executive branch in OECD member countries, 2014**

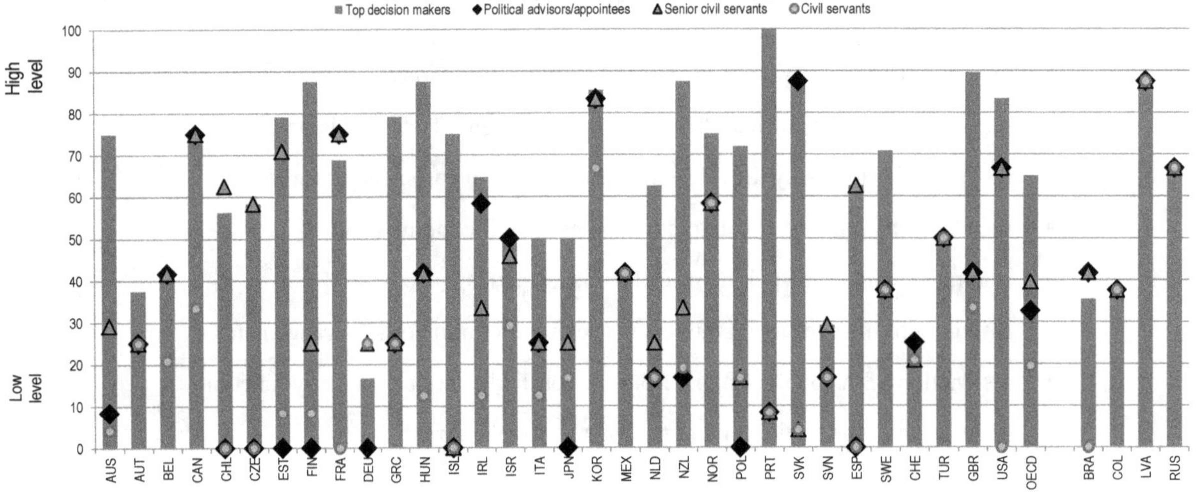

Source: OECD (2015b), *Government at a Glance 2015*, OECD Publishing, Paris, http://dx.doi.org/10.1787/gov_glance-2015-en.

Note: The statistical data for Israel are supplied by and under the responsibility of the relevant Israeli authorities. The use of such data by the OECD is without prejudice to the status of the Golan Heights, East Jerusalem and Israeli settlements in the West Bank under the terms of international law.

Furthermore, the disclosure forms should be both verified for their completeness and reviewed for accuracy. Among OECD countries, ten countries, including Canada, France, Korea and Switzerland, verify receipt of the submitted disclosure form, verify that all required information was included and audit or review the accuracy of the information submitted in the disclosure form for all those required to disclose private interests. In contrast, Colombia only verifies the receipt of the submitted form for all those required to disclose private interests and verify that all required information was included only for some disclosure forms. The verification of submission or review of disclosure forms does not directly result in resolution of potential or actual conflicts of interest but it can effectively prevent potential conflicts of interest. Colombia could consider implementing additional measures regarding the disclosed information, such as verifying for completeness and accuracy, in order to increase effectiveness of the private interest disclosures.

Box 2.11. **Financial disclosures and conflicts of interest: State of Illinois, United States**

The Financial Disclosures and Conflicts of Interest form ("form") must be accurately completed and submitted by the vendor, parent entity(ies), and subcontractors. There are nine steps to this form and each must be completed as instructed in the step heading and within the step. A bid, offer, or proposal that does not include this form shall be considered non-responsive. The agency/university will consider this form when evaluating the bid, offer, or proposal or awarding the contract. The form is divided into eight steps, as follows:

- Step 1. Supporting documentation submittal
- Step 2. Disclosure of financial interest or board of directors
- Step 3. Disclosure of lobbyist or agent
- Step 4. Prohibited conflicts of interest
- Step 5. Potential conflicts of interest relating to personal relationships
- Step 6. Explanation of affirmative responses
- Step 7. Potential conflicts of interest relating to debarment and legal proceedings
- Step 8. Disclosure of current and pending contracts

The requirement of disclosure of financial interests and conflicts of interest is a continuing obligation. If circumstances change and the disclosure is no longer accurate, then disclosing entities must provide an updated form. Separate forms are required for the vendor, any parent entity(ies) and any subcontractors.

The full texts for Steps 4 and 5 are included in Annex 2.A1.

Source: State of Illinois (n.d.), "Financial Disclosures and Conflicts of Interest V.15.2", www.illinois.gov/cpo/general/Pages/SolicitationandContractTemplates.aspx (accessed 13 June 2015).

Effective enforcement through multi-dimensional approach

An open organisational culture to foster internal reporting and facilitate the detection of wrongdoing

Detection of wrongdoings and breaches play an important role in effective enforcement of conflict-of-interest policies and rules. Often, risks of reprisals or retaliation by managers and colleagues deter internal reporting; such retaliatory measures include dismissal, professional marginalisation, demotion, medical testing or examination and transfer or reassignment. An open organisational culture where public procurement officials are encouraged to report could facilitate detection of misconduct or wrongdoings.

Colombia provides limited protection for whistleblowers through provisions in other laws. The laws include provisions on compensation for unjustified dismissal (Labour

Code of 1950), obligations for public officials to report misconduct of suspected corruption (Law 734 of 2002 and Law 906 of 2004 by means of which the Code of Criminal/Penal Procedure was issued) and prohibition on retaliation against public servants who report cases of corruption (Law 1474 of 2011). The scope of corruption however does not necessarily cover misconduct that could arise from not adequately or appropriately identifying and managing conflicts of interest. Obligation for public officials does not in itself provide for protection against unjust consequences. In this vein, Colombia could include specific provisions in their laws in order to extend the protection to those reporting cases of misconduct, including both public officials as well as other stakeholders in the public procurement cycle, to encourage whistleblowers. For instance, Australia has defined what constitutes a protected disclosure and who will be afforded what kinds of protection under the law (Box 2.12).

Box 2.12. **Disclosable conduct as defined by the Australian Public Interest Disclosure Act 2013**

The Australian Public Interest Disclosure (PID) Act 2013 defines disclosable conduct as conduct (in Australia or in a foreign country) that contravenes the law, that constitutes maladministration, that is an abuse of public trust, that results in wastage of public money, public property, money of a prescribed authority, property of a prescribed authority, or conduct that results in danger (or a risk of danger) to the health or safety of one or more persons or the environment. In addition, disclosable conduct also includes when a public official abuses his or her position as a public official and conduct engaged in by a public official that could, if proved, give reasonable grounds for disciplinary action against the public official.

The Act, specifically:

- removes barriers that prevent people who work, or previously worked in the public sector from speaking up about serious problems that impact on public administration
- ensures that reports of wrongdoing are properly investigated and dealt with
- provides protection to public officials who report allegations of wrongdoing under the PID Act.

Source: Australia's Public Interest Disclosure Act 2013, Part 2 Division 2 Section 29; Department of Human Services (n.d.), "Public Interest Disclosure Act", Australian Government, www.humanservices.gov.au/corporate/about-us/public-interest-disclosure-act.

Currently, *Colombia Compra Eficiente* does not receive complaints and does not investigate possible cases of conflicts of interest, as these are not included in its mandate. In order to foster an open organisational culture, safe and clear reporting channels which are well known throughout the organisation with clear rules and procedures, as well as a description of the protection provided for whistleblowers, should be provided. Colombia could consider establishing a hotline to receive reports of suspected corruption cases as well as misconduct during the public procurement cycle, which needs to be clearly defined in law. If a hotline is established outside of *Colombia Compra Eficiente*, co-ordination between the two need to be carefully designed and implemented for it to function effectively (Box 2.13).

Box 2.13. **Whistleblower hotline in Austria**

In March 2013, the Ministry of Justice set up a whistleblower hotline on the homepage of the Public Prosecutor's Office against Corruption and White Collar Crime. As of September 2013, approximately 590 notifications were submitted via the platform. Only 53 of those notifications were not relevant. The whistleblower hotline has a test phase of two years.

The Federal Ministry of Justice's whistleblowing website enables investigators from the Public Prosecutor's Office against Corruption and White Collar Crime (*Zentrale Staatsanwaltschaft zur Verfolgung von Wirtschaftsstrafsachen und Korruption*, WKStA) to get in direct contact with whistleblowers, with the anonymity of the latter being assured. In that event, the whisteblower is entitled to decide whether he/she would like to remain anonymous or to identify him/herself to the investigators.

Sources: Transparency International (2013), "Whistleblowing in Europe", www.transparency.de/fileadmin/pdfs/Themen/Hinweisgebersysteme/EU_Whistleblower_Report_final_web.pdf; Shoneherr (2013), "Austria: Whistleblower Hotline is Launched Online", www.schoenherr.eu/knowledge/knowledge-detail/austria-whistleblower-hotline-is-launched-online/.

Regular assessment and evaluation of the policy implementation through diagnostic tools

The system for managing conflicts of interest needs to be assessed and evaluated regularly in order to ensure sound performance. It provides evidence-based feedback on the real impacts of the policy and effectiveness of policy measures that could feed into reforming and improving the system. In particular, 56% of the OECD countries reported in 2014 to have employed diagnostic tools to monitor and evaluate the effectiveness of the policy, rules and procedures on conflicts of interest.[2] Many of the diagnostic tools are in the forms of surveys done both internally and by an external audit. In some cases, based on the collected data, the responsible bodies and committees draft a report that gets published on a regular basis.

Colombia collects data on sanctions applied during public procurement activities through the supplier's registry, which is an obligation for all procurement agencies applying sanctions. Additionally, when disciplinary sanctions or fiscal responsibility are declared by the General Inspector Office and the General Comptroller Office, they should be registered within the system as well. This data could be an important source to measure effectiveness and identify the weakness of Colombia's system for managing conflict of interest in public procurement. For instance, it could provide public procurement officials with concrete examples of incidences of actual conflict of interest.

Furthermore, the statistical data could be valuable communication tool for not only the public procurement officials but also for the private sector as well as civil society by communicating the government's effort and commitment based on solid evidence in order to adequately identify and manage conflict of interest. Using the statistical data, which are already available, Colombia could use them as an evidence-based assessment and evaluation tool of their system for managing conflict of interest.

Private sector and civil societies can be an additional watchdog during the public procurement process

Many countries involve the private sector and civil societies in different ways to monitor the public procurement process. Integrity breaches in public procurement are often a two-way street resulting from complex relationships between multiple stakeholders. This signifies that adequate and appropriate identification and management of conflict of interest would not be sufficient through public officials alone. In order to have a sound management system, integrity and accountability standards for bidders should be developed and applied as well. Recognising the detrimental effects of integrity breaches, certain suppliers have developed their own standards and programme to enhance integrity, as it is the case in the US Construction Industry Ethics and Compliance Initiative (CIECI) (Box 2.14) and the South Australian Construction Industry (Box 2.15).

Box 2.14. **The Construction Industry Ethics and Compliance Initiative in the United States**

The Construction Industry Ethics and Compliance Initiative (CIECI) is a non-profit private association that brings together more than 50 companies in the US construction industry to establish a process for the industry to promote integrity and ethical conduct.

The construction industry is the United States' largest industry, ranging from building contractors who construct homes, schools, hospitals, skyscrapers and shopping centres to the heavy construction industry that builds power plants, highways, bridges, airports, dams, water treatment facilities and the like. Vast and diverse, the construction industry consists of architect/engineers, contractors and subcontractors who tend to specialise. The essential goals of the initiative are the advancement of organisational cultures that encourage and support ethical behaviour and compliance with the law, and the sharing of best ethical and compliance practices within the industry.

The Initiative requires each signatory company to pledge to follow six core ethical principles, to adhere to these principles, and to participate in an Annual Best Practices Forum to discuss best ethical and business conduct practices among its members and with representatives from government and other organisations. The core principles are:

- Each member shall have and adhere to a written Code of Business Conduct. The Code shall establish high ethical values and compliance with the law applicable to the US construction industry.
- Each member shall train its personnel as to their personal responsibilities under the Code.
- Each member commits itself to work together toward maintaining open competition in the industry, free of conflicts of interest and undue influences.
- Each member shall be responsible for sharing best ethical and compliance practices in implementing the principles with others.
- Each member shall participate in the Annual Best Practices Forum.
- Each member, through participation in this Initiative, shall be accountable to the public.

Source: CIECI (n.d.), "Construction Industry Ethics and Compliance Initiative", www.ciecinitiative.org/Faqs (accessed 18 June 2015).

Box 2.15. Code of Practice for the South Australia Construction Industry

The Code of Practice for the South Australian Construction Industry and its Implementation Guidelines is a statement of the principles that the industry wants to apply to a range of procedures from project conception and initiation, through tendering and construction, to project completion. The Code of Practice for the South Australian Construction Industry and its Implementation Guidelines aims to: *i)* establish standards of behaviour and standards for the management of relationships between parties in various roles within the industry; and *ii)* introduce reforms as agreed by the industry and by the Government of South Australia. The Code of Practice for the South Australian Construction Industry and its Implementation Guidelines are mandatory on all South Australian Government funded and managed construction projects.

The Code was initiated by the private sector of the State's construction industry as part of the ongoing process of industry development. It is a tool to assist the industry to be nationally competitive by strengthening the best practices that already exist and by introducing new best practices. The Code supports the introduction of asset management policies by the Government of South Australia and the achievement of these delivery standards by the private sector.

The main objectives of the Code are to: *i)* promote action to improve efficiency and productivity; *ii)* eliminate unacceptable practices including those that result from short term and expedient decision making; *iii)* establish standards which the industry requires to be observed; *iv)* improve performance and maintain good practice of all participants in the South Australian Construction Industry; *v)* promote the highest standards within the construction industry by seeking the commitment of all those covered by this Code to comply with the full spirit and intent of all laws, regulations and standards applying to the industry; *vi)* obtain the best value by sharing risks equitably through assigning each risk to the party most able to bear the risk; *vii)* promote the application of sensible and proper practices for the long-term benefit of the industry and all parties involved; *viii)* seek to secure improvements in practice that have been achieved so far; *ix)* seek to promote goodwill in the industry and prevent disputes by observing agreements, statutory requirements and obligations of employment.

Source: Government of South Australia (2012), "Code of Practice for the South Australian Construction Industry", www.infrastructure.sa.gov.au/BuildingManagement/policies (accessed 6 May 2015).

Colombia has developed Pro Ethics Records project in order to promote integrity in the private sector, which include a set of international ethical standards and transparency in the private sector, training of employees, collective action and measure to regulate the relationship between the public and private sectors. However, the main targets of the project are big companies and the level of compliance is estimated to be highly costly for small and medium-sized enterprises (SMEs). In this light, Colombia could further reinforce the impact of the project by extending the aforementioned measures to the private sector and involving the private sector, including SMEs, and civil societies in the development of the project, for example in forms of dialogue or surveys.

In order to avoid conflict of interest during the construction of the New International Airport in Mexico City, the Minister of Transport and Communication (SCT) has developed the following template documents:

- **Declaration of possible conflict of interest**: This document must be presented and signed by the public official in charge of the procurement procedure.
- **Survey on anti-corruption practices for the contracts on public works**: This document needs to be completed and signed by the bidder. It includes questions on the knowledge on anti-corruption legal framework; if investigations and/or

sanctions have been applied to the bidder; the existence of internal anti-corruption policy and if the bidder paid bribes to participate in the bid.

- **Template for the declaration of integrity**: This document must be signed by the bidder.

Colombia could develop similar documents and publish them on line to make bidders more accountable.

Citizens and civil society in public procurement are essential, for they can play a role of "direct social control" on government activities. Not only can they play the role of oversight and monitoring, but involving citizens and civil societies in consultation could further increase transparency in government activities, and aid in restoring public trust. In this light, Colombia could greatly benefit from inviting and involving citizens and civil societies throughout the public procurement cycle, as is done, for example, in Mexico in the form of social witnesses (Box 2.16).

Box 2.16. **Social witnesses in Mexico**

Mexico is one of the first OECD countries to have introduced such controls through the involvement of social witnesses in the procurement processes, who are legally required to participate in all stages of public tendering procedures above certain thresholds. In 2015, these thresholds are MXN 350 million (approximately USD 23 million) for goods and services and MXN 710 million (approximately USD 47 million) for public works.

Social witnesses are elected by the Ministry of Public Administration (*Secretaría de la Función Pública*, SFP) through public tendering and when a federal entity requires the involvement of a social witness, SFP designates one from the preselected pool. Following their participation in procurement procedures, social witnesses issue a final report providing comments and recommendations on the process. These reports must subsequently be published on the Mexican federal e-procurement platform (CompraNet).

Source: OECD (2015a), *Effective Delivery of Large Infrastructure Projects: The Case of the New International Airport of Mexico City*, OECD Public Governance Reviews, OECD Publishing, Paris, http://dx.doi.org/10.1787/9789264248335-en.

Recommendations

- Colombia could benefit from clarifying conflict of interest regime in their laws by including a proper definition of conflict-of-interest situations.
- Colombia could develop a specific conflict-of-interest policy for procurement officials.
- Colombia could develop a code of conduct for procurement officials and for those involved in the procurement process, including suppliers, bidders, subcontractors and temporary staff, not covered by public officials rules.
- Colombia could greatly benefit from providing dedicated and systematic ethics or integrity trainings that are offered on a regular basis, and eventually extending the training to more stakeholders, including suppliers and contractors.

- *Colombia Compra Eficiente* could consider implementing additional declaration and evaluation steps prior to preclusion of the bidders from the process.
- Colombia could consider including in their approach options for positive resolution or management of conflict of interest for public procurement officials.
- Colombia could benefit from implementing a more tailored approach to disclosure and public availability requirements concerning the public officials' private interests who are exposed to more risks of conflict of interest.
- Colombia could consider implementing additional measures regarding the disclosed information, such as verifying for completeness and accuracy, in order to increase effectiveness of the private interest disclosures.
- Colombia could include specific provisions in their laws in order to extend the protection to those reporting cases of misconduct, including both public officials as well as other stakeholders in the public procurement cycle, to encourage whistleblowers.
- Colombia could consider establishing a hotline to receive reports of suspected corruption cases as well as misconduct during public procurement cycle, which needs to be clearly defined in law. If the hotline is established outside of *Colombia Compra Eficiente*, co-ordination between the two need to be carefully designed and implemented for it to function effectively.
- Colombia could develop "Declaration of possible conflict of interest" and a "Declaration of integrity" and publish them on line to make bidders more accountable.
- Colombia could use the statistical data collected on sanctions and fiscal responsibilities through different systems as an evidence-based assessment and evaluation tool of their system for managing conflict of interest.

Notes

1. Such conflicts of interest are mentioned in, for instance, Articles 23, 36, 40, Item 17 of 48 and 50 of Colombia Disciplinary Code (Law 734 of 2002) as well as Article 8 of the Procurement Law, which states specific prohibitions arising from conflicts of interests in the context of public contracts.
2. Based on the 32 OECD countries' responses to the 2014 OECD Survey on Managing Conflict of Interest in the Executive Branch and Whistleblower Protection.

References

Bowman J. B. (1990), "Ethics in government: a national survey of public administrators", Public Administration Review, 345-353. Bowman, J. B. and R. L. Williams (1997), "Ethics in government: from a winter of despair to a spring of hope", Public Administration Review, 57(6), 517-526. CCAB, (2014), "Developing and implementing a code of ethical conduct", www.ccab.org.uk/PDFs/Code_Guidance_final_SG_Amends2.pdf (accessed 18 June 2015).

CIECI (n.d.), "Construction Industry Ethics and Compliance Initiative", www.ciecinitiative.org/Faqs (accessed 18 June 2015).

Department of Human Services (n.d.), "Public Interest Disclosure Act", Australian Government, www.humanservices.gov.au/corporate/about-us/public-interest-disclosure-act (accessed 18 June 2015).

Department of Planning, Transport and Infrastructure (DPTI) (n.d.), "Procurement Management Framework: Confidentiality and Conflict of Interest", PR115, Australian Government, http://dpti.sa.gov.au/__data/assets/pdf_file/0015/114351/PR115 Confidentiality_and_Conflict_of_Interest.pdf (accessed 16 June 2015).

Flake R. and J.A. Grob (1998), "The nature and scope of state government ethics codes, Public Productivity and Management Review, 21(4), 453-459.

Gilman S.C. and C.W. Lewis (1996), "Public service ethics: a global dialogue", Public Administration Review, 56(6), 517-524. Government of South Australia (2012), "Code of Practice for the South Australian Construction Industry", www.infrastructure.sa.gov.au/BuildingManagement/policies (accessed 6 May 2015).

Integrity Coordinating Group (2011), "Conflicts of Interests Guidelines for the Western Australia Public Sector", https://icg.wa.gov.au/sites/default/files/documents/Conflicts__%20of%20interest%20-%20Guidelines%20for%20the%20WA%20public%20_sector.pdf (accessed 6 May 2015).

Integrity Coordinating Group (n.d.), "Conflicts of interest - guidelines and scenarios", https://icg.wa.gov.au/node/81 (accessed 6 May 2015).

National Audit Office (2015), "Conflicts of interest", Report by the Comptroller and Auditor General, Session 2014-15, 27 January, www.nao.org.uk/wp-content/uploads/2015/01/Conflicts-of-interest.pdf (accessed 28 January 2016).

OECD (2015a), *Effective Delivery of Large Infrastructure Projects: The Case of the New International Airport of Mexico City*, OECD Public Governance Reviews, OECD Publishing, Paris, http://dx.doi.org/10.1787/9789264248335-en.

OECD (2015b), *Government at a Glance 2015*, OECD Publishing, Paris, http://dx.doi.org/10.1787/gov_glance-2015-en.

OECD (2014), "Survey on Managing Conflict of Interest in the Executive Branch and Whistleblower Protection".

OECD (2013a), *OECD Integrity Review of Italy: Reinforcing Public Sector Integrity, Restoring Trust for Sustainable Growth*, OECD Public Governance Reviews, OECD Publishing. http://dx.doi.org/10.1787/9789264193819-en.

OECD (2013b), "Ethics training for public officials", brochure, www.oecd.org/corruption/acn/library/EthicsTrainingforPublicOfficialsBrochureEN.pdf.

OECD (2007), *Integrity in Public Procurement: Good Practice from A to Z*, OECD Publishing, Paris, http://dx.doi.org/10.1787/9789264027510-en.

OECD (2004), *Managing Conflict of Interest in the Public Service: OECD Guidelines and Country Experiences*, OECD Publishing, Paris, http://dx.doi.org/10.1787/9789264104938-en.

Public Works and Government Services Canada (PWGSC) (n.d.), "The Code of Conduct for Procurement", www.tpsgc-pwgsc.gc.ca/app-acq/cndt-cndct/contexte-context-eng.html (accessed 17 June 2015).

Reed, Q. (2008), "Sitting on the fence: Conflicts of interest and how to regulate them", *U4 ISSUE* 2008:6.

Shoneherr (2013), "Austria: Whistleblower Hotline is Launched Online", 29 April, www.schoenherr.eu/knowledge/knowledge-detail/austria-whistleblower-hotline-is-launched-online/ (accessed 13 June 2015).

State of Illinois (n.d.), "Financial Disclosures and Conflicts of Interest V.15.2", www.illinois.gov/cpo/general/Pages/SolicitationandContractTemplates.aspx (accessed 13 June 2015).

Stewart D.W. and N.A. Sprinthall (1993), "The impact of demographic, professional, and organisational variables and domain on the moral reasoning of public administrators". H.G. Frederickson (ed.), Ethics and public administration (pg. 205-219), New York: M.E. Sharpe Inc.

Transparency International (2014) "Implementing codes of conduct in public institutions", www.transparency.org/whatwedo/answer/implementing_codes_of_conduct_in_public_institutions

Transparency International (2013), "Whistleblowing in Europe", www.transparency.de/fileadmin/pdfs/Themen/Hinweisgebersysteme/EU_Whistleblower_Report_final_web.pdf (accessed 13 June 2015).

Treasury Board Code of Values and Ethics (2006), "Conflict of Interest Act", Canada, www.tbs-sct.gc.ca/pol/index-eng.aspx?|=V.

UK Government (2015), "The Public Contracts Regulations 2015", www.legislation.gov.uk/uksi/2015/102/pdfs/uksi_20150102_en.pdf (accessed 13 June 2015).

Annex 2.A1

Financial disclosures and conflicts of interest: State of Illinois, United States

STEP 4
PROHIBITED CONFLICTS OF INTEREST
(All vendors must complete regardless of annual bid, offer, or contract value)
(Subcontractors with subcontract annual value of more than $50,000 must complete)

Step 4 must be completed for each person disclosed in Step 2, Option A and for sole proprietors identified in Step 1, Option 6 above. Please provide the name of the person for which responses are provided:

1. Do you hold or are you the spouse or minor child who holds an elective office in the State of Illinois or hold a seat in the General Assembly? ☐ Yes ☐ No

2. Have you, your spouse, or minor child been appointed to or employed in any offices or agencies of State government and receive compensation for such employment in excess of 60% ($106,447.20) of the salary of the Governor? ☐ Yes ☐ No

3. Are you or are you the spouse or minor child of an officer or employee of the Capital Development Board or the Illinois Toll Highway Authority? ☐ Yes ☐ No

4. Have you, your spouse, or an immediate family member who lives in your residence currently or who lived in your residence within the last 12 months been appointed as a member of a board, commission, authority, or task force authorized or created by State law or by executive order of the Governor? ☐ Yes ☐ No

5. If you answered yes to any question in 1-4 above, please answer the following: Do you, your spouse, or minor child receive from the vendor more than 7.5% of the vendor's total distributable income or an amount of distributable income in excess of the salary of the Governor ($177,412.00)? ☐ Yes ☐ No

6. If you answered yes to any question in 1-4 above, please answer the following: Is there a combined interest of self with spouse or minor child more than 15% in the aggregate of the vendor's distributable income or an amount of distributable income in excess of two times the salary of the Governor ($354,824.00)? ☐ Yes ☐ No

STEP 5
POTENTIAL CONFLICTS OF INTEREST RELATING TO PERSONAL RELATIONSHIPS
(Complete only if bid, offer, or contract has an annual value over $50,000)
(Subcontractors with subcontract annual value of more than $50,000 must complete)

Step 5 must be completed for each person disclosed in Step 2, Option A and for sole proprietors identified in Step 1, Option 6 above.

Please provide the name of the person for which responses are provided:

1.	Do you currently have, or in the previous 3 years have you had State employment, including contractual employment of services?	☐ Yes ☐ No
2.	Has your spouse, father, mother, son, or daughter, had State employment, including contractual employment for services, in the previous 2 years?	☐ Yes ☐ No
3.	Do you hold currently or have you held in the previous 3 years elective office of the State of Illinois, the government of the United States, or any unit of local government authorized by the Constitution of the State of Illinois or the statutes of the State of Illinois?	☐ Yes ☐ No
4.	Do you have a relationship to anyone (spouse, father, mother, son, or daughter) holding elective office currently or in the previous 2 years?	☐ Yes ☐ No
5.	Do you hold or have you held in the previous 3 years any appointive government office of the State of Illinois, the United States of America, or any unit of local government authorized by the Constitution of the State of Illinois or the statutes of the State of Illinois, which office entitles the holder to compensation in excess of expenses incurred in the discharge of that office?	☐ Yes ☐ No
6.	Do you have a relationship to anyone (spouse, father, mother, son, or daughter) holding appointive office currently or in the previous 2 years?	☐ Yes ☐ No
7.	Do you currently have or in the previous 3 years had employment as or by any registered lobbyist of the State government?	☐ Yes ☐ No
8.	Do you currently have or in the previous 2 years had a relationship to anyone (spouse, father, mother, son, or daughter) that is or was a registered lobbyist?	☐ Yes ☐ No
9.	Do you currently have or in the previous 3 years had compensated employment by any registered election or re-election committee registered with the Secretary of State or any county clerk in the State of Illinois, or any political action committee registered with either the Secretary of State or the Federal Board of Elections?	☐ Yes ☐ No
10.	Do you currently have or in the previous 2 years had a relationship to anyone (spouse, father, mother, son, or daughter) who is or was a compensated employee of any registered election or reelection committee registered with the Secretary of State or any county clerk in the State of Illinois, or any political action committee registered with either the Secretary of State or the Federal Board of Elections?	☐ Yes ☐ No

Source: State of Illinois (n.d.), *"Financial Disclosures and Conflicts of Interest V.15.2"*, www.illinois.gov/cpo/general/Pages/SolicitationandContractTemplates.aspx (accessed 13 June 2015).

Chapter 3

Evaluation criteria to award contracts in the Colombian public procurement system

This chapter examines the use of available tender procedures and evaluation criteria to award contracts in the Colombian public procurement system. These issues entail the distribution of public resources to private entities, and are important not only because decisions that are made during this process can be harmful for the integrity of the procurement process but also because they can lead to waste of public funds if they are not carried out in a transparent and equitable manner. The focus of this chapter is therefore on the criteria for selecting procurement methods and the criteria for awarding a certain bid a contract. There is special focus on direct awarding and the mechanism that is in place to support secondary objectives.

A sound evaluation framework produces equitable results

In order to have a competitive, effective and sound tender and awarding process the OECD (2015a) "Recommendation of the Council on Public Procurement" (hereafter, the "OECD Recommendation") states that countries should "facilitate **access** to procurement opportunities for potential competitors of all sizes". Furthermore, under this principle the OECD Recommendation states that countries should " [...] *ii)* **Deliver clear and integrated tender documentation, standardised where possible and proportionate to the need**, [...] and *iii)* **Use competitive tendering and limit the use of exceptions and single-source procurement**."

It is important to properly prepare the public procurement process from the early stages, providing a suitable set of conditions, including adequate evaluation and award criteria that will allow for equitable results from the bidding process. To achieve that:

> "specific tender opportunities should be designed so as to encourage broad participation from potential competitors, including new entrants and small and medium-sized enterprises. This requires providing clear guidance to inform buyers' expectations (including specifications and contract as well as payment terms) and binding information about evaluation and award criteria and their weights (whether they are focused specifically on price, include elements of price/quality ratio or support secondary policy objectives),"
>
> and, on the other hand,
>
> "the extent and complexity of information required in tender documentation and the time allotted for suppliers to respond should be proportionate to the size and complexity of the procurement" (OECD, 2015a).

Finally, the nature of the procurement process may affect the expected outcomes in many aspects and that is why "competitive procedures should be the standard method for conducting procurement as a means of driving efficiencies, fighting corruption, obtaining fair and reasonable pricing and ensuring competitive outcomes. If exceptional circumstances justify limitations to competitive tendering and the use of single-source procurement, such exceptions should be limited, pre-defined and should require appropriate justification when employed, subject to adequate oversight, taking into account the increased risk of corruption, including by foreign suppliers."

Procurement methods: Theory and reality

Competitive tendering enhances transparency in the procurement process and provides equal opportunities and access to potential suppliers. Government officials, however, must determine the optimum procurement strategy that balances concerns for administrative efficiency with competition and fair access for suppliers.

Colombian procurement laws permit public government groups to utilise five different types of procurement procedures depending upon certain circumstances, factors and exceptions: *i)* public tenders; *ii)* an abbreviated selection process (for example, for routine, standardised products); *iii)* a selection based on qualifications/merit (used for consultancy services where price is not the main consideration and cannot be legally considered); *iv)* a direct selection or award; and *v)* a low-value contract process. Suppliers responding to a procurement selection process are required to submit a bid bond (usually 10% of the value of the budgeted amount for the contract). Ordinarily, firms awarded a contract must submit a performance bond to guarantee their compliance with the obligations of the contract, although this is not a requirement with respect to low-value contracts (*de mínima cuantía*). Colombian public procurement agencies may extend the scope of a contract provided that the increased value of the contract does not exceed 50% of the initial value of the contract. According to the Colombian procurement authorities, the general rule is to conduct competitive processes with open tender being the default option. However, various established exceptions allow for the use of other approaches.

The merit contest is the mechanism utilised to select consultants. Abbreviated selection method is the option for standardised goods and services but also where the objective of the selection is based on the products to be contracted, the circumstances of the contract, the amount or the destination of goods and services. For procurement below a specified amount (*mínima cuantía*) small scale procurement is the option. Direct awarding is allowed in the following cases: *i)* manifest urgency; *ii)* loan agreements; *iii)* agreements between government agencies (including agreements to undertake jointly the mission of government agencies as well as the actual business between government agencies and state-owned enterprises which affect open competition); *iv)* goods and services for the defence government agencies that require keeping data in reserve; *v)* trust agreements to be entered into by the subnational level when agencies have started a reorganisation of debts proceeding; *vi)* when there is no plurality of bidders; *vii)* for personal professional services to support the operations of the government agency; *viii)* lease and sale of real estate. When discretion in selecting a contracting method is available, contracting officials should evaluate both the nature of the procurement as well as broader procurement objectives.

Information collected through SECOP (*Sistema Electrónico de Contratación Pública*) and the e-shop TVEC (*Tienda Virtual del Estado Colombiano*) show an enormous increase in the amount and number of public procurement contracts between 2012 and 2014, both at national and sub-national level. The cause of this increase is most likely the result of the enforcement of the mandatory obligation to publish contract information by the contracting authorities on these two platforms and not necessarily[1] the result of a massive increase in the volume of public procurement in Colombia. In fact, according to *Colombia Compra Eficiente* (CCE), the data presented in Tables 3.1 and 3.2 reflect about 75-80% of the total procurement volume in 2014. The value of reported contracts has doubled between 2012 and 2014 though the increase in the number of contracts has only increased by 20%.

There was a similar amount of increase at the sub-national level between 2012 and 2014. Even though 60% of the total value of contracts is at the national level, 75% of the total contracts are made at the sub-national level. The main explanation for the number of contracts at the sub-national level is the huge amount of direct awards that are close to 300 000 in total (see Table 3.2). Most of them are for personal professional services, i.e. hiring of staff.

Table 3.1. **Value and number of procurement contracts at a national level in Colombia, per type of contract, 2012 and 2014**

Type of contract	Value of contracts, 2014, in USD millions	Value of contracts, 2012, in USD millions	Number of contracts, 2014	Number of contracts, 2012
Public-private partnership	4 640.813	0.000	9	
Open merit competition	274.486	217.314	951	507
Merit competition with a short list	1.554	41.778	4	150
Direct awarding	6 315.465	4 815.493	107 209	89 221
Contracting with minimum budget	260.690	273.706	38 076	44 009
Public tender	3 344.445	2 512.615	1 622	1 603
Special regime	7 016.137	2 261.675	32 188	11 946
Abbreviated selection with low budget	854.779	542.670	4 652	4 601
Abbreviated selection article H	27.212	122.083	49	46
Abbreviated selection health services	205.337	0.028	326	1
Auction	510.655	984.485	2 489	2 127
Demand aggregation	118.924	0.000	888	
Minimum amount	0.728	0.000	76	
Total	23 571.227	11 771.848	188 539	154 211

1. Currency exchange: COP 1.00 = USD 0.000343080, 30 October 2015.

Source: Information collected through SECOP (*Sistema Electrónico de Contratación Pública*) and the e-shop TVEC (*Tienda Virtual del Estado Colombiano*) for 2012 and 2014. Provided by the Government of Colombia to the OECD Secretariat during a mission, 19-22 May 2015.

Table 3.2. **Value and number of procurement contracts at a sub-national level in Colombia, per type of contract, 2012 and 2014**

Type of contract	Value of contracts, 2014, in USD millions	Value of contracts, 2012, in USD millions	Number of contracts, 2014	Number of contracts, 2012
Public-private partnership	0.116	0.524	4	6
Open merit competition	326.352	95.049	3 584	1 278
Merit competition with a short list	3.621	23.508	67	154
Merit competition with multipurpose list	1.391	4.658	7	21
Direct awarding	6 308.525	4 020.246	299 419	180 435
Contracting with minimum budget	450.133	344.596	94 370	86 739
Public tender	5 049.591	1 530.382	6 232	2 032
Special regime	2 472.717	1 065.888	117 650	13 149
Abbreviated selection with low budget	1 008.578	371.357	9 233	6 418
Abbreviated selection article H	22.844	7.098	88	47
Abbreviated selection health services	17.847	14.792	113	73
Auction	620.288	261.400	4 466	2 768
Demand aggregation	15.446	0.000	154	
Minimum amount	0.058	0.000	17	
Total	16 297.508	7 738.975	535 404	293 120

1. Currency exchange: COP 1.00 = USD 0.000343080, 30 October 2015.

Source: Information collected through SECOP (*Sistema Electrónico de Contratación Pública*) and the e-shop TVEC (*Tienda Virtual del Estado Colombiano*) for 2012 and 2014. Provided by the Government of Colombia to the OECD Secretariat during a mission, 19-22 May 2015.

The decision to use a procedure with limited competition or direct awarding is not subject to approval at a level higher than the contracting official. Despite the need to justify the procedure, the number of reasons allowing for direct awarding in Colombia make it a common method to use. In reality, 60% of contracts in Colombia are awarded through direct awarding at a national and sub-national level. It is important to note that the special regime contracts are not subject to the procurement statute but are funded by the government. Since 2013 the activity of the aggregation of demand instruments has been listed under aggregation TVEC as well as contracting goods under the *minima cuantía* procedure.

The Colombian government contracting regime calls for the use of tenders as the preferred method for the procurement of goods and services by its public procurement entities. However, Tables 3.1 and 3.2 demonstrate that the vast majority of public sector contracts in Colombia are awarded through direct awarding and that several other selection processes are more often used than public tenders. The OECD recognises the importance for public procurement agencies to be permitted the flexibility to purchase via direct awards in the case of small-value contracts or purchases that are best sourced locally for resource, time and cost reasons. However, the overall value of public tenders, at both national and sub-national level is only about 20% of total contract value and less than 1% of all procurement contracts made in Colombia in 2014. More in-depth analysis of direct award follows in the next section of this chapter.

The Colombian framework to public procurement has been set up in line with the traditional procurement cycle, starting with procurement planning and proceeding in sequence to need assessment, advertising, invitation to bid, prequalification, bid evaluation (broken down further into technical and financial evaluation), post-qualification, contract award and contract implementation. The methods used in Colombia are broadly in line with procurement procedures in Europe, which mainly differ on the level of competition they create. Box 3.1 provides a brief overview of some of the most common public procurement methods used today.

Box 3.1. **Common procurement methods**

Open procedure: This procedure is the most commonly used public procurement procedure among EU states. In contrast to other procedures, the bidding is open to all interested suppliers, including cross-border bidders.

Restricted procedure: This procedure proceeds in two stages: First the tender is advertised with fairly broad requirements in which suppliers are invited to express interest. Second, the contracting authority invites a limited number of qualified suppliers to submit a detailed offer.

Negotiated procedure: The contracting authority (CA) has the opportunity to directly select bidders that will then participate in the tender procedure. The CA invites candidates to submit offers and negotiate the terms of the contract with them. The contract is then awarded to the technically compliant tender who offers best value for money. The method is used in a small number of cases.

Competitive dialogue: This procedure is used when the CA is unable to either specify technical means of satisfying their needs or to specify the legal or financial set up of the project. The CA publishes the contract notice and then opens a dialogue with the candidates satisfying the selection criteria as stated in the contract. The contract is then awarded to the technically compliant tender who offers best value for money.

Simplified procedure and direct award: When the value of a contract is below specific thresholds (defined at national level), procurement procedures can be simplified.

Source: EU Commission (2015), "Stock-taking of administrative capacity, systems and practices across the EU to ensure compliance and quality of public procurement involving European Structural and Investment (ESI) Funds", progress report.

The OECD Recommendation states that "rules for justifying and approving exceptions to procurement procedures should be comprehensive and clear, such as in cases of limiting competition." It is also recommended that competitive (open) procedures should be the standard method for conducting procurement as a means of driving efficiencies, fighting corruption, obtaining fair and reasonable pricing and ensuring competitive outcomes. If exceptional circumstances justify limitations to competitive tendering and the use of single-source procurement, such exceptions should be limited, pre-defined and should require appropriate justification when employed, subject to adequate oversight taking into account the increased risk of corruption, including by foreign suppliers. See Box 3.2 for examples of exception processes used by countries.

Box 3.2. **Use of exceptions to competitive bidding in public procurement**

To ensure a level playing field, exceptions to competitive bidding shall be strictly defined in order to avoid abuse. Also, governments should consider setting up procedures to introduce transparency and integrity measures for exceptions to competitive tendering. Assessment of countries shows that:

- Written justification for the use of non-competitive tendering procedures is required in almost all respondent countries.
- Random reviews or audits of non-competitive procedures are required in three-quarters of respondent countries.
- A higher level of authorising personnel is required for non-competitive tenders in half of respondent countries.
- Fewer countries require that the amendments to contracts be made publicly available or to provide independent validation for large or high-value procurement (30% of respondent countries).

Source: OECD (2013a), *Implementing the OECD Principles for Integrity in Public Procurement: Progress since 2008*, OECD Public Governance Reviews, OECD Publishing, Paris, http://dx.doi.org/10.1787/9789264201385-en.

The standards set by the OECD on exceptions from competitive tendering call for more thorough analysis on behalf of the CCE. There is a need for clear and specific criteria for justifying the limitation of competition. The main challenge for the CCE for the next few years is too confront the excessive use of non-competitive procurement methods by agencies at the national and sub-national level. The CCE should develop specific criteria for evaluating whether a specific tender is eligible for exception and that criteria should be objective, transparent and equitable. There is a need for a better monitoring mechanism; either with a committee or a centralised decision-making body like the CCE, that can approve limitations to competitions at a higher level; hence it would no longer be in the hands of local contracting officials.

There have been significant improvements in the reporting of contract information and CCE needs to continue to enforce the publication of contract information. Informing all relevant parties about the latest legal amendments, explaining what they entail and then enforcing them is a task that the CCE needs to adhere to. Steps have been taken to improve the legal framework for public procurement in Colombia, including direct awarding. However, the legal framework does not adequately cover the sub-regional level.

The weight of direct awarding and the risks of non-competitiveness

Most Colombian procurement processes do not involve public tenders; they utilise direct awards or involve only a few select participants. Procedures other than public tenders usually undermine transparency in public procurement and they tend to focus on easing the workload of procurement officials rather than on the functional performance of the goods and services to be procured, as suggested by the 2012 OECD "Recommendation of the Council on Fighting Bid Rigging in Public Procurement" (OECD, 2014a). According to Colombian legislation, procurement agencies have to justify, at the level of the contracting official, the basis for conducting a direct awarding.[2] The criteria to justify the limitation of competition shall be linked with the cause that authorises the direct awarding.

The Government of Colombia has been cleaning up its procurement data to enhance the reliability of the information on the size of the procurement market and the total number, type (products, works and services) and value of contracts. Also, the CCE has been leading the drafting of a bill to pass a new law to, among other things, consolidate, clarify and reduce the grounds on which direct awards can be made. It will place an obligation on buying entities to justify recourse to direct award, to identify clearly the rationale for the direct award and follow specific conditions and rules of procedure for direct awards. The number of exceptions for using direct awards in Colombia is presented in Table 3.3. Inappropriate use of direct awarding should be viewed as the most serious breach of procurement rules and should result in the contract being declared ineffective and the imposition of very severe sanctions under the remedies regime.

Table 3.3. **Exceptions for direct awarding in Colombia**

Manifest urgency	Declaration, urgency, manifestation
Loan agreements	Loan, "bank interest"
Agreements between government agencies	All direct awarding entities signed by the Defence sector, National Intelligence Agency and the National Protection Unit
Goods or services for the development of activities science and technology	Software, scanning, license , platform, database, research, innovation
Professional services and support management or artistic works that can only be entrusted with certain people	Management support, technical, "labour", services, professionals, doctor, specialist, consultant, consulting, consulting, composer, composition, music, musician, artist
Purchasing property	Purchase, acquisition
Real estate leasing	Lease , leasing property

Source: World Bank (2015a), *"Contratación directa en Colombia: Elementos de derecho internacional y consideraciones empíricas sobre su prevalencia"*, World Bank Group.

According to the study carried out by CCE with the World Bank, where the objective was to understand the limits to competition caused by the use of direct awarding, the frequency of its usage is mainly associated with the defence sector and professional services (hiring of staff) at the national level (Figure 3.1). Professional services account for more than half of all direct awarding in Colombia. This situation results from the existence of inherited restrictions in the budget norms limiting the increase in personnel expenses for public servants in Colombia. That reduces the ability of public institutions to have a flexible and proactive policy. In order to overcome these constraints, many public entities use the direct award of professional services to compose their workforce and as a tool of human resource management. At the sub-regional level the professional services category alone is responsible for over 80% of the exceptions, potentially indicating the need to assess what expertise is maintained among the civil service and what is outsourced to contractors. It is important to make clear that exceptions to competitive tendering should not be abused to procure daily military equipment when national interests are not at stake.

Although most contracts are concluded by direct awarding, the value of public procurement is also concentrated in other types of contracts, in particular contracting with minimum budget and special regimes. However, based on available information, approximately USD 8.8 billion in 2012 and USD 12.5 billion in 2014 were through direct awarding, which shows the importance of this type, not only in the volume of contracts but in all public procurement (World Bank, 2015b).[3] Figure 3.2 presents the composition of reasons for direct awards by sector in Colombia. The use of professional services is almost dominant in all sectors except for the defence and law enforcement sectors.

The use of direct awarding is not an isolated characteristic of the Colombian public procurement system. In many international jurisdictions this is a common practice (see Figure 3.3). The framework for exceptions in Colombia from competitive tendering is not abnormal. The number of legislative acts that allow for direct awarding to take place in Colombia is on par with Australia, similar to the EU average level and a bit lower than the United Kingdom and Mexico. There are however legitimate reasons for concern about the excessive use of exceptions in Colombia.

In the past it has been far too easy for government agencies in Colombia to use exceptions from the competitive tendering process. This is supported by comprehensive data on public procurement in Colombia and by the information gathered during the fact-finding mission. What the Colombian government has been trying to do since the CCE was established in 2012 is commendable. However, recent legislation doesn't go far enough in prohibiting the use of exceptions and it also doesn't give the CCE enough authority to improve the procurement process at the sub-national level.

CCE should investigate the use of exceptions for direct awarding on a regular basis in order to identify opportunities to improve the planning and management of its procurement function and reduce such occurrences. While such practices are recommended, only 47% of the countries that responded to the 2012 OECD Survey require assessments or audits to evaluate *ex post* the use of exceptions for direct awards of contracts at the central government level. Of those who do, 33% undertake them on an ad hoc basis (OECD, 2013b).

Reducing the number of exceptions for direct awarding through legislative changes will have an impact. However, the problem goes deeper than that in Colombia. There is an institutional and a systemic problem that has led the public sector to circumvent conventional recruitment processes. Hence, there is an over-reliance on hiring staff through the professional service scheme. This gives a distorted picture of the cost of employment and productivity in the public sector.

The opportunity for increasing the effectiveness of the public sector by strategically using procurement methods has not been seized. More should be done to create a competitive real estate market for the public sector. The government needs to look more thoroughly at the needs of the state for government buildings and how the size of available offices can be used more productively. There is potential for great savings by using competitive tendering or reverse auctions for purchasing property or leasing real estate.

Figure 3.1. **Frequency of the use of exceptions to carry out direct awards in Colombia, 2013**

National level

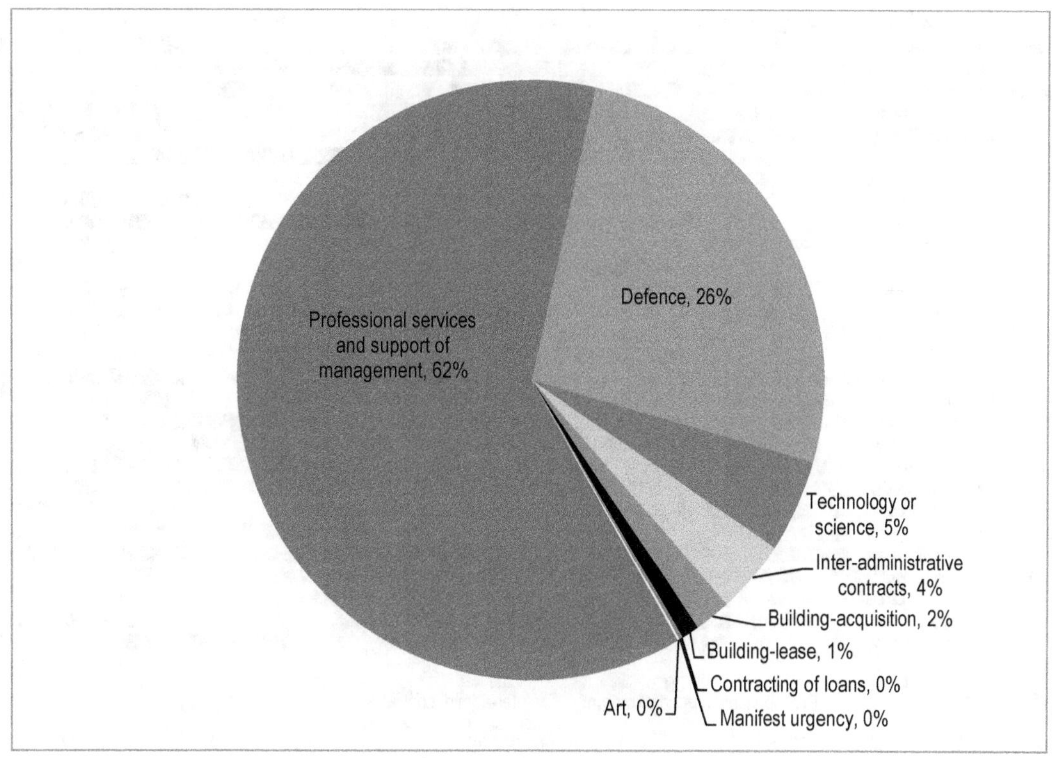

Sub-regional level

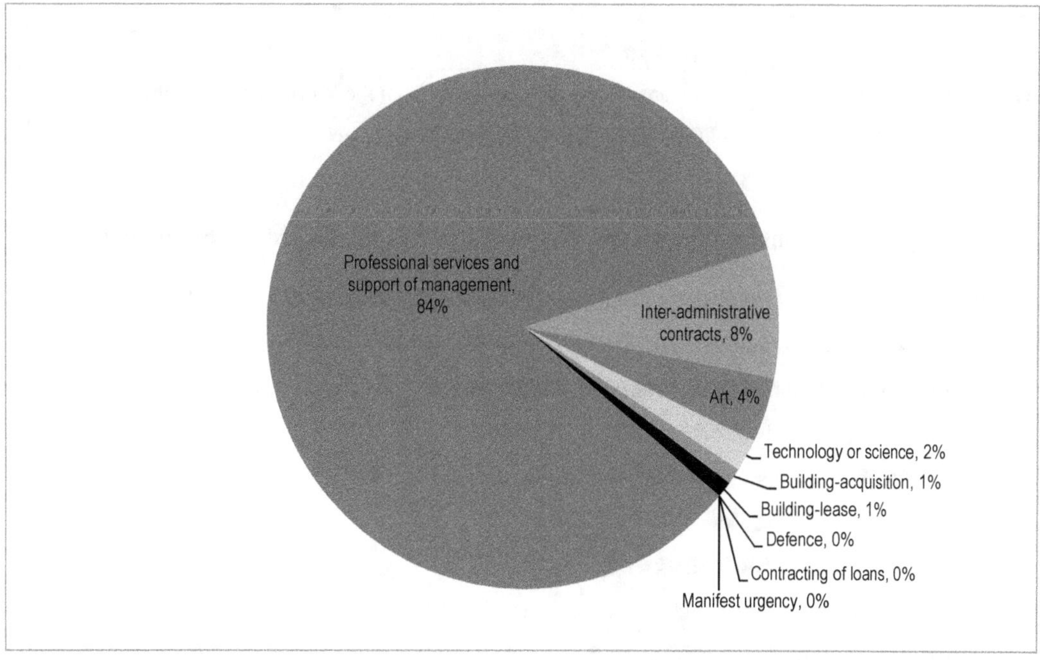

Note: The numbers used to reproduce the figure are rough estimates taken from the World Bank (2015b).

Source: World Bank (2015b), *"Estudio de política pública sobre prácticas de contratación y competencia en Colombia"*, World Bank Group.

Figure 3.2. **Composition of the reasons for direct awards by sector, by Colombia's National Central Government (*Gobierno Nacional Central*, GNC)**

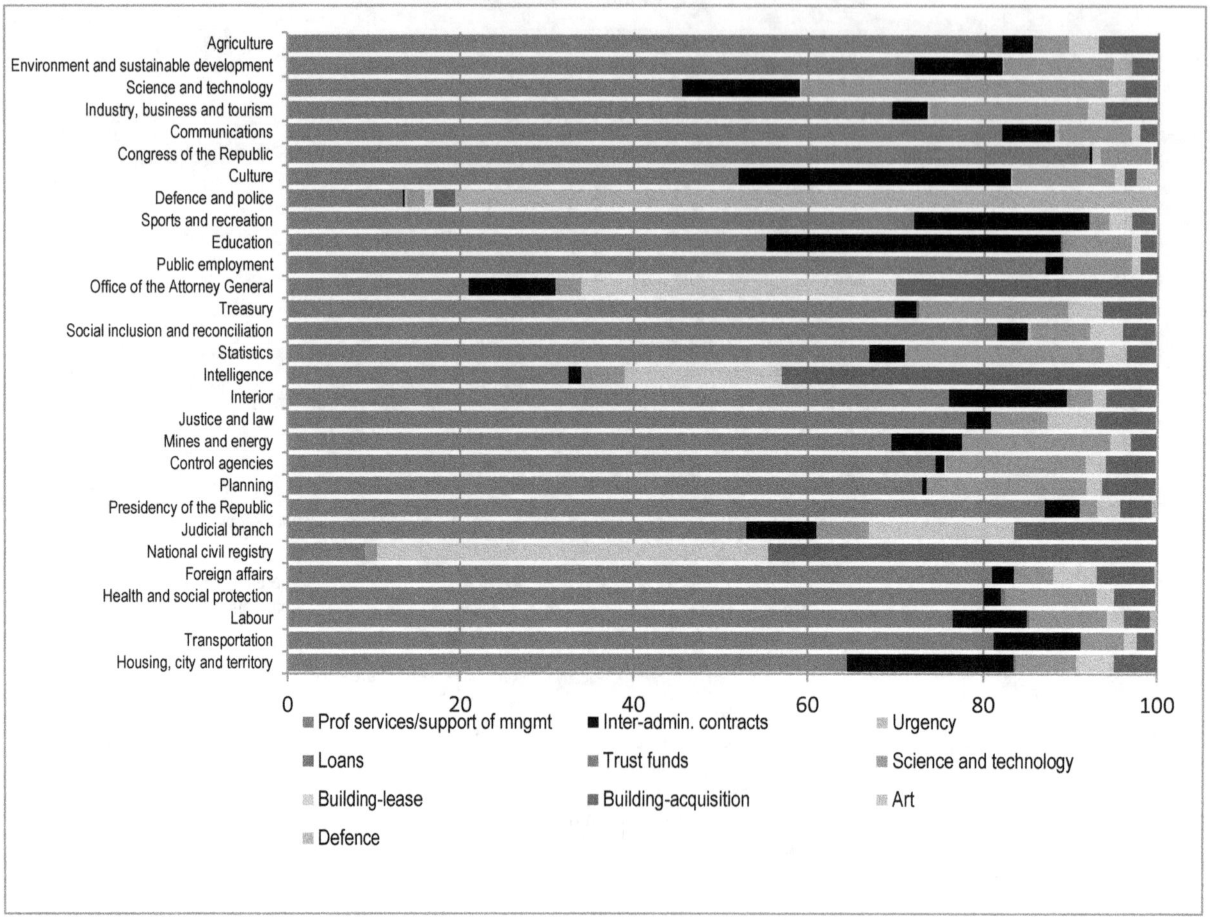

Agriculture
Environment and sustainable development
Science and technology
Industry, business and tourism
Communications
Congress of the Republic
Culture
Defence and police
Sports and recreation
Education
Public employment
Office of the Attorney General
Treasury
Social inclusion and reconciliation
Statistics
Intelligence
Interior
Justice and law
Mines and energy
Control agencies
Planning
Presidency of the Republic
Judicial branch
National civil registry
Foreign affairs
Health and social protection
Labour
Transportation
Housing, city and territory
0
20
40
60
80
100
Prof services/support of mngmt
Inter-admin. contracts
Urgency
Loans
Trust funds
Science and technology
Building-lease
Building-acquisition
Art
Defence

Note: The numbers used to reproduce the figure are rough estimates taken from the World Bank (2015b).

Source: World Bank (2015b), *"Estudio de política pública sobre prácticas de contratación y competencia en Colombia"*, World Bank Group.

Figure 3.3. **Number of legislative acts permitting direct awarding, by country**

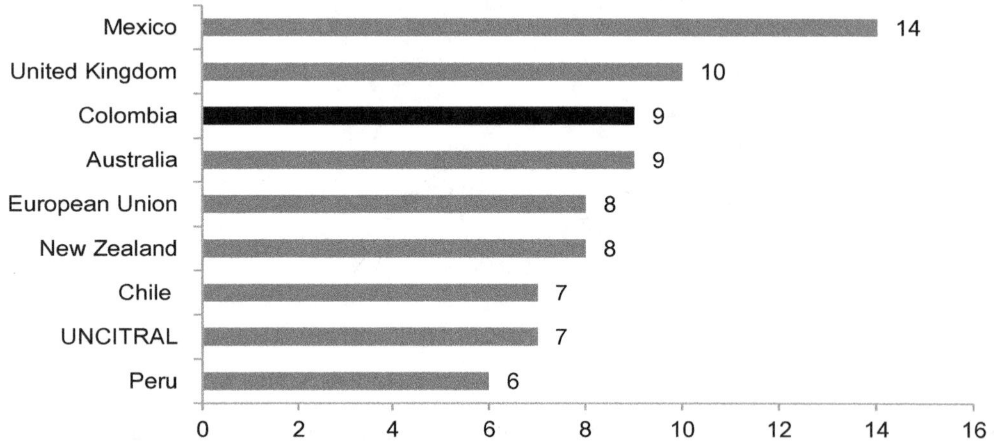

Mexico
14
United Kingdom
10
Colombia
9
Australia
9
European Union
8
New Zealand
8
Chile
7
UNCITRAL
7
Peru
6
0
2
4
6
8
10
12
14
16

Source: World Bank (2015b), *"Estudio de política pública sobre prácticas de contratación y competencia en Colombia"*, World Bank Group.

Towards a more holistic selection framework

Colombian regulation provides guidelines for the objective selection of contractors, including: *i)* legal power and capacity; *ii)* experience; *iii)* best value, understood as favourable offer bearing in mind technical and economic aspects; *iv)* lower price; *v)* specific experience of the bidder and its team. Open tender procedure is based on price and on additional technical aspects. There are two types of merit contests: a prequalification (*lista corta*) based on experience and background of the equipment of the bidder (education, publications, etc.), and an open one. There are five types of abbreviated selection: *i)* lower value; *ii)* standardised goods and services; *iii)* the procurement from government agencies taking care of personal protection of threatened people, *iv)* the procurement from the government agency tasked with demobilisation of persons from guerrilla groups, *v)* attention to violence victims; goods and services for national defence and health services. Selection process with small budget (*mínima cuantía*) is based on price.

The amounts to define small scale procurement (*mínima cuantía*) and to define when the abbreviated selection process is correspondent are linked with the budget of the procurement agency in five ranges expressed in monthly legal minimum wages that are updated on yearly basis. Small scale procurement are in amounts below USD 26 000 and USD 7 200, depending on the budget of the procurement agency and abbreviated selection is below USD 260 000 and USD 26 000, also depending on the budget of the procurement agency. The procurement agency in the bid terms shall define the evaluation criteria based in the guidelines set forth in the applicable regulation.

In the European Union some states have a single national threshold for supplies and services. A few of these countries require that EU rules, with limited simplification, be followed above these thresholds, whilst others are not prescriptive about the procedures to be followed. The starting point for national thresholds below which direct procurement can take place varies considerably. See examples in Table 3.4.

Table 3.4. **Examples of starting points for national thresholds for direct awarding**

Thresholds				
Less than USD 16 400	Ranges between USD 22 000-USD 33 000	Less than USD 43 000	Less than USD 73 000	Less than USD 76 400
Bulgaria, Cyprus, Finland, France, Latvia, Poland, Romania and Slovenia	Italy, Hungary, Lithuania and the Slovak Republic	Austria and Estonia	Denmark	Czech Republic

Source: OECD (2010), "Public Procurement in EU Member States - The Regulation of Contract Below the EU Thresholds and in Areas not Covered by the Detailed Rules of the EU Directives", *Sigma Papers*, No. 45, OECD Publishing, http://dx.doi.org/10.1787/5km91p7s1mxv-en.

Note by Turkey: The information in this document with reference to "Cyprus" relates to the southern part of the Island. There is no single authority representing both Turkish and Greek Cypriot people on the Island. Turkey recognises the Turkish Republic of Northern Cyprus (TRNC). Until a lasting and equitable solution is found within the context of the United Nations, Turkey shall preserve its position concerning the "Cyprus issue".

Note by all the European Union Member States of the OECD and the European Union: The Republic of Cyprus is recognised by all members of the United Nations with the exception of Turkey. The information in this document relates to the area under the effective control of the Government of the Republic of Cyprus.

All selection criteria affect the intensity and effectiveness of competition in the tender process. The decision on what selection criteria to use is not only important for the current project, but also in maintaining a pool of potential credible bidders with a continuing interest in bidding on future projects. It is therefore important to ensure that qualitative selection and awarding criteria are chosen in such a way that credible bidders, including small and medium-sized enterprises (SMEs), are not deterred unnecessarily. Pre-selection procedures should verify the qualifications of potential contractors or suppliers, including professional and technical qualifications, managerial capacity, financial resources, and the legal capacity to enter into a procurement contract.

It is a common working practice for governments around the world, at a national or sub-national level, to encourage contracting officials to award contracts to the lowest bidder as this is seen as the safest course of action from transparency and public perception perspectives. Public buyers have a similar tendency because it is the easiest method of awarding contracts. However, this method is an overly simplistic approach to procurement. Also, it can make bid rigging more likely to occur as it makes the public procurement procedures more predictable. Bid rigging works best when the procurement criteria are continuously based on selecting the lowest priced bid in the selection processes. This is an additional reason why it is important that Colombian policy makers and procurement officials recognise the importance of non-price factors such as quality, service, delivery terms, payment terms, warranties, etc. and permit the use of such selection criteria in awarding contracts (OECD, 2014a).

Colombian procurement statutes require government purchasing groups to undertake a “preliminary study” before they commence a procurement process.[4] In the past, such studies have largely dealt with the nature of the procurement and procurement process and the intended contractual terms and conditions so they were not true market studies. Article 15 of the recently enacted Decree 1510 of 2013 now specifically requires Colombian government officials to undertake a market analysis before a procurement process is commenced purchasing. Despite these legislative changes few public procurement officials in Colombia prepare market studies and or have the skills to carry out such a study. To address this issue, CCE established the minimum acceptable content for market studies through a manual published in 2013 and updated in 2014, which can be used by Colombian procurement agencies when they undertake their market studies (CCE, 2014a). The purpose of market studies is set out in Box 3.3.

Box 3.3. **Market studies**

Market studies are vitally important and a valuable preparatory tool. They should be undertaken even when there is no legal requirement to do so, particularly so for tenders of large value. A thorough understanding of all prevailing market conditions and potential suppliers is essential, if contracting authorities want to both buy effectively and detect and avoid bid rigging.

Market studies should identify the characteristics and specifications of the:

- goods and services to be purchased
- existing and potential suppliers
- alternative products
- price trends over time
- differences in prices between private and public procurement markets
- costs and other competitive variables.

Market studies should be conducted by individuals with procurement and/or research expertise, who are provided with sufficient time and resources.

Source: OECD (2014a), “Fighting Bid Rigging in Public Procurement in Colombia: A Secretariat Report on Colombian Procurement Laws and Practices”, www.oecd.org/daf/competition/Booklet_SIC%20Procurement%20Report_16X23_REV_web.pdf.

The Colombian procurement system is fairly decentralised with more than 4 400 public purchasing entities at the central and sub national levels. There are several challenges that need to be addressed to improve the management of public entities. During the fact-finding mission it was found that many procurement agencies do not have the organisational capabilities to be effective managers of procurement procedures. The knowledge required for effective management is not well used; it is dispersed throughout organisations and not properly and cohesively co-ordinated inside them. There is dispersion of authority, attention is too focused on the issue of the day and not on long-term solutions or the issues the organisation is allegedly in charge of. The corporate culture of most organisations is not supportive of innovation.

It is important to acknowledge the efforts made by the Colombian authorities to enhance the skills of procurement staff. However, there are significant competency gaps that prevent public agencies from optimising the procurement process. Such gaps relate both to core procurement activities (e.g. market research, knowledge of the procurement legal framework and use of diversified evaluation and selection methods in competitive tendering) and to the general management of the function and its risks (e.g. identification and management of potential risks, conflict of interest and wrongdoing, as well as middle manager management skills). There has been a need for a training strategy for procurement officials. No standard training or certification is provided to all procurement officers, and determining competency gaps and training requirements is left to each procurement unit. Attending a training course is not compulsory and there are no incentives to do so other than personal motivation. Most procurement officials develop knowledge and capability mostly through experience, resulting in an unevenly qualified workforce. The CCE is now in the process of developing a training programme which needs to be accessible to both national and subnational level.

Framework for evaluation and awards

The bid evaluation has been considered a particularly vulnerable step. A key concern is the lack of transparency when using economic, social and environmental criteria to evaluate bidders (e.g. favouring bidders from economically disadvantaged areas, using environmentally friendly materials, etc.). In Colombia the criteria to select the contractor or supplier depend on the selection process mode. However, the regulation provides incentives for SMEs, the handicapped population and national industry. They are set forth in the terms and conditions (sustainable procurement or local buying) by the procurement agency. In addition, the government has promoted including incentives for sustainable procurement in the terms of reference, which has been used in the framework agreements promoted by CCE. The incentives are secondary to the main evaluation criteria. Colombian procurement agencies have to set up a points system as part of the evaluation criteria and give in accordance to such incentives.

The possibility to conclude framework agreements in Colombia has been allowed by law since 2007. However the procedure was not used commonly until CCE was put in charge of setting up framework agreements, updating and overseeing the electronic procurement platform. CCE encourages the use of framework agreements to aggregate demand for products and services commonly required across government entities and assist in the standardisation of such purchases. The task of setting up such agreements for commonly procured products and services is assigned to CCE. The role of central purchasing bodies (CPB) like CCE is very important for the successful implementation of framework agreements (see other CPB examples in Box 3.4).

Box 3.4. **Framework agreements: The role of the central purchasing body**

Most centralised purchase bodies such as Consip in Italy or PPS in Korea design and carry out framework agreements. Framework agreements are a procurement technique that allows purchasers to buy under a pre-established "umbrella" agreement.

Consip is the Italian national central purchasing body established in 2000 under the form of a state-owned company entirely owned by the Ministry of Economy and Finance (MEF). Its main goal is to run framework agreements and bulk purchasing for standardised goods and services for all public administrations, especially central administrations, and to manage the public electronic marketplace for low-value and non-standardised purchases. Italy estimates that public administrations achieve cost savings of 27% through the use of framework agreements.

In Korea, the PPS undertook research of the arrangements for framework agreements in several countries with developed public procurement systems. On the basis of that research the implementation of multiple award schedules (MAS) began in January of 2005. Korean framework agreements serve as a model that achieves the benefits of centralised purchasing while remaining open to encourage competition, avoiding a common pitfall of such arrangements.

As a centre of efficiency, PPS serves the role of a central purchasing body, and implements many good practices. The success of PPS is demonstrated by the fact that use of PPS' purchasing services continues to increase, despite the fact that mandatory use of these services by local and other entities has been phased out over time.

A range of items that are usually covered by framework agreements:

- ICT products and services (computers, photocopiers, printers, servers, software), generally the largest product area in terms of purchasing volume
- telecommunications products (networks, mobile phones, landline phones, telephone exchanges)
- office furniture
- travel services
- office equipment and supplies
- vehicle and transport services
- fuel (for heating and transport) and electricity
- food (foodstuffs, meal tickets)
- organisational and human resources development services.

Source: OECD (2014b), *Spain: From Administrative Reform to Continuous Improvement*, OECD Public Governance Reviews, OECD Publishing, http://dx.doi.org/10.1787/9789264210592-en; OECD (2016), *The Korean Public Procurement Service: Innovating for Effectiveness*, OECD Public Governance Reviews, OECD Publishing, Paris, http://dx.doi.org/10.1787/9789264249431-en.

One of the main objectives of the CCE 2012-13 Action Plan was to use framework agreements as a way to tap into the potential of aggregating demand and on the development of an electronic platform to promote standardisation of procurement practices. The CCE has tried to increase the awareness of CCE and its success is likely to depend on the extent to which trust and confidence can be built and maintained in its relations with major stakeholders, i.e. end users of framework agreements. Under the Decree 1510/2013, the use of framework agreements was made compulsory for buying entities at the central government level and optional for subnational buyers. More in-depth analysis of secondary objectives follows in the next section of this chapter.

Regulations on how to use these criteria together with other evaluation criteria has to be clear to prevent harming the integrity of the public procurement process. Even when the evaluation criteria are defined in a transparent and precise manner, they usually offer discretion to evaluators. If bidders are to trust and respect the outcome, they need to know how discretion was exercised and how criteria were applied (OECD, 2007). It is important to be aware of the risks involved as conflict-of-interest situations can lead to bias and corruption in the evaluation and in the approval process. OECD recommends "binding information about evaluation and award criteria and their weights (whether they are focused specifically on price, include elements of price/quality ratio or support secondary policy objectives" (OECD, 2015a).

In Colombia, procurement authorities have set standards for the proposals evaluation criteria. Procurement agencies are supposed to be objective and base their evaluation on prices, technical matters or best value. For the award process, agencies are supposed to establish the weight of price and technical aspects in the bidding terms and explain the basis for these assigned weights in the preliminary studies. This is however not always the case, even though CCE has issued the following instruments to assist the procurement agencies with their evaluation:

1. A manual to guide procurement agencies in their definition of the criteria required of the private sector to allow them to participate in selection processes (*requisitos habilitantes*).
2. A manual for small-scale procurement available.
3. Standard bidding documents for public works to be executed with resources from the national level, including an appendix for the evaluation criteria (CCE, 2014a, 2014b and 2014c).

There are protections to ensure that bid evaluation is conducted in line with the criteria and selection method identified in the tender documents. The procurement agency shall publish the evaluation report before awarding the contract and the bidders may file comments and questions thereof. In addition, the bidders may solve issues related to their offers that are not part of the elements used to compare bidder offers any time before the award. The evaluations shall be conducted in accordance with the bid terms guaranteeing equal treatment and an objective selection of the best offer; otherwise, procurement agencies and officers may be liable. To ensure equal treatment and symmetry of information for potential bidders during the preparation and evaluation of bids, all government agencies in Colombia shall publish at SECOP all its procurement activity to offer the same information to all interested parties to guarantee equal treatment. See Box 3.5 for an example of objective criteria for evaluating awards.

Box 3.5. **Objective award criteria**

Ensure that award criteria are clearly and objectively defined by:

i) using evaluation criteria on the basis of the economically most advantageous, unless this is a commodity purchase for which the basis of the lowest price may be used

ii) specifying the relative weightings of each criteria and justifying them in advance

iii) specifying to what extent these considerations are taken into account in award criteria when using economic, social or environmental criteria

iv) including any action that the procuring agency is entitled to make in the criteria (such as negotiations, under what conditions, etc.) and recording them.

Source: OECD (2009), *OECD Principles for Integrity in Public Procurement*, OECD Publishing, Paris, http://dx.doi.org/ 10.1787/9789264056527-en.

Colombian procurement agencies may have evaluation committees, but they are not obliged to do so. Usually the procurement process of significant value has evaluation committees in place and there are many procurement agencies that have it. The conflict-of-interest regime is applicable to the members of the committee. The procurement agency shall publish the results of the evaluation in SECOP. Procurement agencies are liable for mistakes in the evaluation and officers may be personally liable therefore. It is important for CCE to clarify the procedures for the use of evaluation committees. Civil society may comment on the documentation of the procurement process, and in particular on the evaluation report, as well as participate in the hearings to allocate risks, and the award hearing as well as the performance of the contract. Colombian Political Constitution (Article 270) states that the law shall organise a system of citizen participation in public affairs to oversee public management and its results have been named citizen control, exercised by an individual or a group of individuals who form an institution, called *veeduría.*

The Government of Colombia has been investing in procurement to increase transparency and effectiveness. It is vitally important to continue on that path to ensure the integrity of the public procurement cycle. There is still opportunity for improvement and with SECOP II, the new electronic procurement platform, some of the most significant challenges that the Colombian authorities are facing could be solved. The electronic procurement system should provide the Government with more reliable data on procurement, increase transparency and accountability. However, the system is decentralised and many key decisions concerning the bidding process are in the hands of employees, some with limited experience in procurement. A more concrete evaluation framework is needed, both for the bids and committees. This could involve verifying that officials in charge of the evaluation are not in a conflict-of-interest situation (e.g. through mandatory disclosure) and are bound by confidentiality requirements. In the case of an evaluation committee, integrity and professional considerations must be taken into account in the selection of members, and involve a member external to the procurement team when possible.

Strategically supporting secondary objectives through the awarding mechanism

In recent years governments have been increasingly using their purchasing power as a policy lever to support various secondary objectives, such as green growth, the development of small and medium-sized enterprises, or innovation. The OECD has monitored these trends since 2012, as well as in the development of public procurement data for the *OECD Governance at a Glance*, 2013 and 2015. Moving from primary objectives, where the aim is to achieve value for money and ensure timely and efficient procurement of goods and services is not without its controversy as it is the taxpayer's money that is being spent. The framework surrounding procurement with secondary objectives can be quite complicated to implement. The disqualification of bidders due to their not meeting certain social or environmental requirements can reduce competition and be more costly to both the suppliers and the state depending on the case. Despite these hindrances, changes in public procurement laws have been moving towards a more accommodating outlook towards environmental and social objectives.[5]

The Government of Colombia has had a strong social focus in the past, setting out incentives in regulations for the support of SMEs, national industry and disabled people. More recently the Government decided to promote green procurement by setting environmental objectives. The National Development Plan (*Plan Nacional de Desarollo para Todos*) 2010-14 prioritises sustainable production and processes and optimal use of natural resources. To promote these objectives, in 2012 the Colombian Ministry of Environment collected information on environmentally sustainable public procurement and selected five products (coffee; printed materials including books, maps and publications; light bulbs; paper; and mining materials) on which it is conducting market research in order to arrive at environmental procurement targets (e.g. product specifications, selection criteria). Alongside such market research, the Ministry of Environment has issued 15 guidelines on how to include green criteria in procurement, five of which include lifecycle analysis of products. The likelihood of success of such green procurement projects will to an extent depend on the adoption of adequate monitoring mechanisms to assess their progress and results (OECD, 2013b).

The OECD encourages a balanced approach to the inclusion of policy goals in public procurement. Recognising the delivery of goods and services necessary to accomplish government missions in a timely, economical and efficient manner as the primary procurement objective, the OECD Recommendation identifies secondary policy objectives as any of a variety of objectives pursued through public procurement, such as sustainable green growth, the development of small and medium-sized enterprises, innovation, standards for responsible business conduct or broader industrial policy objectives. The policy choice regarding whether to pursue secondary policy objectives in public procurement will vary by government and the needs of citizens, but the OECD Recommendation identifies steps that should be taken whenever such objectives are pursued (see Box 3.6).

Box 3.6. **OECD Recommendation on secondary policy objectives**

V. RECOMMENDS that Adherents recognise that any use of the public procurement system to pursue secondary policy objectives should be **balanced** against the primary procurement objective.

To this end, Adherents should:

i) Evaluate the use of public procurement as one method of pursuing secondary policy objectives in accordance with clear national priorities, balancing the potential benefits against the need to achieve value for money. Both the capacity of the procurement workforce to support secondary policy objectives and the burden associated with monitoring progress in promoting such objectives should be considered.

ii) Develop an appropriate strategy for the integration of secondary policy objectives in public procurement systems. For secondary policy objectives that will be supported by public procurement, appropriate planning, baseline analysis, risk assessment and target outcomes should be established as the basis for the development of action plans or guidelines for implementation.

iii) Employ appropriate impact assessment methodology to measure the effectiveness of procurement in achieving secondary policy objectives. The results of any use of the public procurement system to support secondary policy objectives should be measured according to appropriate milestones to provide policy makers with necessary information regarding the benefits and costs of such use. Effectiveness should be measured both at the level of individual procurements, and against policy objective target outcomes. Additionally, the aggregate effect of pursuing secondary policy objectives on the public procurement system should be periodically assessed to address potential objective overload.

Source: OECD (2015a), "Recommendation of the Council on Public Procurement", www.oecd.org/corruption/recommendation-on-public-procurement.htm.

The vast majority of OECD member countries use public procurement as a tool to implement policies or strategies to foster secondary policy objectives. In fact, 26 OECD member countries have developed strategies or policies to support green public procurement, SMEs and innovative goods and services. These strategies are predominantly developed at the central level (see Table 3.5). In sharp contrast, the number of OECD member countries that report measuring the results of their strategies or policies to promote environmental or socio-economic objectives is significantly lower and exhibits differences between the policy objectives. Among the 26 OECD member countries who have a strategy or policy developed at the central level or by procuring entities (line ministries), 18 (69%) measure the results of their strategy or policy to support green public procurement. Just 15 OECD member countries (58%) measure the results of their strategy or policy to support SMEs. Only 9 OECD member countries (35%) measure the impact of their policy or strategy to foster innovative goods and services.

Table 3.5. **Development of strategic public procurement in OECD countries, by objective**

	Green public procurement	Support to SMEs	Support to innovative goods and services
Australia	●	●	●
Austria	●	○	●
Belgium	♦●	●	●
Canada	♦●	●	●
Chile	♦●	♦●	●
Denmark	●	●	●
Estonia	○	○	○
Finland	●	♦	♦
France	♦●	♦●	♦●
Germany	●	●	●
Greece	♦●	●	○
Hungary	♦	●	●
Ireland	●	●	●
Italy	♦	♦	♦
Japan	●	●	●
Korea	●	●	●
Luxembourg	♦●	♦●	♦
Mexico	●	●	●
New Zealand	♦●	♦●	♦●
Norway	◘	♦●	♦●
Poland	●	●	●
Portugal	●	♦	♦
Slovak Republic	○	○	○
Slovenia	♦●	●	●
Spain	♦●	♦●	♦●
Sweden	♦●	●	●
Switzerland	♦●	♦●	♦
United Kingdom	●	●	●
United States	●	●	♦●
Brazil	♦●	♦●	●
Colombia	♦	●	●
OECD 29			
♦ A strategy / policy has been developed by some procuring entities	13	10	10
● A strategy/policy has been developed at a central level	24	23	20
◘ A strategy / policy has been rescinded	1	0	0
○ A strategy/policy has never been developed	2	3	3

Source: OECD (2015b), *Government at a Glance 2015*, OECD Publishing, Paris, http://dx.doi.org/10.1787/gov_glance-2015-en.

Colombian authorities have taken positives steps in recent years to incorporate social and environmental criteria for awarding contracts into its procurement process. It is now for example compulsory to have award criteria that takes into consideration national industries and disabled people.[6] Proposing green policies, practices and methods is also now a part of the current CCE strategy. Despite legislative improvements, there is a lack of comprehensive data on the impact and success of these measures. There are also concerns that an overly detailed regulatory framework prevents potential suppliers like SMEs from participating in the procurement process, as it is not easy to follow the rules.

Assessment and monitoring mechanisms are useful to assess and consolidate the benefits of secondary objectives and feedback into the planning, setting of criteria and awareness steps. In Canada, to verify the implementation of the Policy on Green Procurement, government agencies are required to publish in their year-end performance reports a section on progress made in implementing these objectives (OECD, 2013a). CCE should set up a framework for measuring results of the strategies/policies to use procurement to support socio-economic or environmental objectives. Part of that framework should include assessments of the extent to which public procurement is used in practice to support socio-economic or environmental objectives in Colombia compared to other methods.

Proposals for action

The Colombian procurement regulations allow for too many exceptions to competitive public tendering. The procurement method that is considered most likely to install trust and transparency in the Colombian procurement process is almost non-existent. Various explanations have been identified during the review process and in the interviews with procurement staff and stakeholders in Colombia.

Procurement agencies base their selection to a large extent on the lowest cost. This approach may be legitimate for the acquisition of standard goods, as it facilitates the evaluation and selection process while ensuring that minimum requirements are met. However, a selection method based only on price may result in various negative impacts for the organisation, such as lower quality, unsecure supply and unsatisfactory supplier performance. It also does not consider the overall costs of use and disposal of the equipment (unless a lifecycle approach is used) and other benefits to the organisation.

The CCE has gradually been introducing new methods as framework agreements into the procurement toolbox. Now it is obligatory for buying entities at the central level to use framework agreements but it is still optional for sub-national byers to use it. The enforcement of the framework agreements need to go further as it is now the prerogative of procurement agencies to assess whether framework agreements fulfil their needs or not.

Recommendations

- Restructure the public procurement process by promoting simplification and standardisation of the tendering process. The lack of standardisation of documents and templates through paper tendering or e-tendering does not allow for potential efficiency gains to be fully exploited. Simplifying and standardising different local tendering procedures and documents would reduce risk and improve interoperability.

- Increase competition by: *i)* reducing the occurrences of contract splitting and the use of exceptions to public tendering; *ii)* increasing whenever possible the participation of foreign suppliers; *iii)* increasing consolidation efforts; *iv)* using reversed auctions; and *v)* improving market research to be aware of all available solutions to the requirements.
- Undertake sufficient discussions with the various procurement agencies at national and sub-national level to ensure that all information and lessons learned developed internally is considered in the development of specific organisation-wide procurement strategies and assess *ex post* their impact.
- Create a knowledge network to increase professionalism of public procurement. This would facilitate the management and dissemination of good practices, knowledge, crossing the boundaries between practices, science, law and policy, between governments and markets, as well as among countries.
- Increase the use of flexible contractual vehicles providing efficiencies and higher savings such as framework agreements, multi-year contracts and contracts with options. This should include the regular assessment and communication of the benefits and outcomes (e.g. saving) achieved under them. Promote the use of a larger range of evaluation and selection criteria (including lifecycle cost assessments).
- Provide more consistent and regular training to procurement experts and suppliers (particularly small and medium-sized enterprises). Use other development methods to improve the skills of the procurement workforce, including knowledge sharing and team-based learning, coaching and mentoring.
- Ensure adequate capacity, in particular at the sub-national level, by employing and training procurement professionals, using collaborative procurement mechanisms, and employing e-procurement tools. There is a need to promote professionalisation and procurement as a specific profession at the sub-national level. Maximise transparency, establish clear accountability and ensure competitiveness by mandating the sub-national level to abide by national set procurement rules.

Notes

1. Decree 1510 of 2013 and Circular 1 of 2013 issued by CCE, see http://sintesis.colombiacompra.gov.co/sites/default/files/20150406_decree_1510_of_2013.pdf and www.colombiacompra.gov.co/sites/default/files/normativas/20130621circular1publicacionensecop.pdf.
2. Paragraph 1 of Article 2 of Law 1150 of 2007 and Article 73 of Decree 1510 of 2013.
3. Currency exchange: COP 1.00 = USD 0.000343080, 30 October 2015.
4. Pursuant to Article 25 of Law 80 of 1993, Article 2.1.1 of Decree 734 of 2012 and Article 15 of Decree 1510 of 2013.
5. EU Public Sector Directive 2014/24/EU and Utilities Directive 2014/25/EU.
6. Benefits for enterprises that hire handicapped persons (Law 361 of 1997 - Article 4.2.5.5 - www.secretariasenado.gov.co/senado/basedoc/ley/1997/ley_0361_1997.html).

References

CCE (*Colombia Compra Eficiente*) (2014a), "Guía para la Elaboración de Estudios de Sector", www.colombiacompra.gov.co/sites/default/files/manuales/cce_guia_estudio_sector_web.pdf.

CCE (2014b), "Manual para determinar y verificar los requisitos habilitantes en los Procesos de Contratación", www.colombiacompra.gov.co/sites/default/files/manuales/20140901_manual_requisitos_habilitantes_4_web.pdf.

CCE (2014c), "Apéndice de requisitos habilitantes – documentos tipo de obra pública contratos plan", www.colombiacompra.gov.co/sites/default/files/manuales/20140828apendicecontratosplan_0.pdf

EU Commission (2015), "Stock-taking of administrative capacity, systems and practices across the EU to ensure compliance and quality of public procurement involving European Structural and Investment (ESI) Funds", progress report.

OECD (2016), *The Korean Public Procurement Service: Innovating for Effectiveness*, OECD Public Governance Reviews, OECD Publishing, Paris, http://dx.doi.org/10.1787/9789264249431-en.

OECD (2015a), "Recommendation of the Council on Public Procurement", www.oecd.org/corruption/recommendation-on-public-procurement.htm.

OECD (2015b), *Government at a Glance 2015*, OECD Publishing, Paris, http://dx.doi.org/10.1787/gov_glance-2015-en.

OECD (2014a), "Fighting Bid Rigging in Public Procurement in Colombia: A Secretariat Report on Colombian Procurement Laws and Practices", www.oecd.org/daf/competition/Booklet_SIC%20Procurement%20Report_16X23_REV_web.pdf.

OECD (2014b), *Spain: From Administrative Reform to Continuous Improvement*, OECD Public Governance Reviews, OECD Publishing, Paris, http://dx.doi.org/10.1787/9789264210592-en.

OECD (2013a), *Implementing the OECD Principles for Integrity in Public Procurement: Progress since 2008*, OECD Public Governance Reviews, OECD Publishing, Paris, http://dx.doi.org/10.1787/9789264201385-en.

OECD (2013b), *Government at a Glance 2013*, OECD Publishing, Paris, http://dx.doi.org/10.1787/gov_glance-2013-en.

OECD (2010), "Public Procurement in EU Member States - The Regulation of Contract Below the EU Thresholds and in Areas not Covered by the Detailed Rules of the EU Directives", *Sigma Papers*, No. 45, OECD Publishing, http://dx.doi.org/10.1787/5km91p7s1mxv-en.

OECD (2009), *OECD Principles for Integrity in Public Procurement*, OECD Publishing, Paris, http://dx.doi.org/10.1787/9789264056527-en.

OECD (2007), *Integrity in Public Procurement: Good Practice from A to Z*, OECD Publishing, Paris, http://dx.doi.org/10.1787/9789264027510-en.

World Bank (2015a), "Contratación directa en Colombia: Elementos de derecho internacional y consideraciones empíricas sobre su prevalencia", World Bank Group.

World Bank (2015b), "Estudio de política pública sobre prácticas de contratación y competencia en Colombia", World Bank Group.

Chapter 4

Accountable public procurement in Colombia

This chapter looks into the role of suppliers and control entities to enforce public procurement law and principles, and prevent and correct irregularities. Ensuring accountable public procurement involves a variety of interrelated controls, which are examined in this chapter. Actions by suppliers include observations before public procurement authorities and legal remedies before the courts. Measures by Colombia's control entities are fiscal and disciplinary.

Introduction and scope of this chapter

To promote accountability in public procurement, the OECD (2015a) "Recommendation of the Council on Public Procurement" (hereafter, the "OECD Recommendation") states that countries should "apply oversight and control mechanisms to support accountability throughout the public procurement cycle, including **appropriate complaint and sanctions processes**" (emphasis added).

Remedies for suppliers include "actions available to economic operators participating in contract award procedures, which allow them to request the enforcement of public procurement regulations and their rights under those regulations in cases where contracting authorities, either intentionally or unintentionally, fail to comply with the legal framework for public procurement" (OECD/SIGMA, 2010). Suppliers are the prime beneficiaries of competitive and lawful procurement procedures, as only such procedures offer them a real and fair chance of winning a contract. Suppliers can be well placed to know whether public procurement procedures are conducted fairly, either because they participate in one, or because they monitor the market to find out about opportunities it offers, and are aware of, or interested in finding out about, their rights. This information, and their interest in seeing their rights complied with, mean that they may be likely to challenge wrongdoing and thus contribute to a more open, transparent and merit-based procurement.

However, they can only do this when adequate courses of action exist. To be effective, a remedies system must be well designed, clear, capable of offering protection in an accessible, uncomplicated, inexpensive and speedy manner. In this respect, the OECD Recommendation provides that countries should "handle complaints in a fair, timely and transparent way through the establishment of effective courses of action for challenging procurement decisions to correct defects, prevent wrong-doing and build confidence of bidders, including foreign competitors, in the integrity and fairness of the public procurement system. Additional key aspects of an effective complaints system are dedicated and independent review and adequate redress." Box 4.1 shows some core requirements for an effective remedies system.

Box 4.1. **Requirements for an effective remedies system**

It is important for suppliers to have remedies available to them to enforce procurement rules. They can be motivated to monitor procurement procedures and require that procurement rules be followed so that their chances of being awarded a contract are not unlawfully diminished. Thus remedies both enhance the lawfulness of procedures as well as encourage competition.

Remedies, so as to be effective, must be:

- clear and straightforward, i.e. understandable and easy to use
- available to all economic operators wishing to participate in a specific contract award procedure without discrimination, in particular on the grounds of nationality
- effective in preventing or correcting instances of unlawfulness on the part of suppliers and/or public authorities.

Source: Adapted from OECD/SIGMA* (2010), "Public Procurement Training for IPA Beneficiaries", Module F: Review and Remedies; Combating Corruption, www.sigmaweb.org/publications/46189707.pdf (accessed 11 August 2015).6

*SIGMA (Support for Improvement in Governance and Management) is a joint initiative of the OECD and the European Union, principally financed by the European Union.

While this chapter focuses on bidder remedies before the procurement contract is concluded (i.e. actions during the public procurement procedure and up until the award decision), it also briefly examines dispute mechanisms during the performance of the contract.

This chapter also looks at the effect of measures taken by control entities in the area of public procurement. In Colombia, the framework governing the public control system is laid down in the Constitution, which establishes external control institutions that are independent from the three branches of government. At the central level, the external control system is made up of the two following bodies:

- The Office of the Comptroller General of the Republic of Colombia (*Contraloría General de la República de Colombia,* the "Contraloría") is an independent institution that acts as the highest level of fiscal control in the country. Its mission is to oversee the proper allocation of public funds (in terms of results achieved through spending and investments) and contributes to the modernisation of the state by means of improvement in fiscal management by various public entities.
- The Office of the Inspector General of Colombia (*Procuraduría General de la Nación*, the "Procuraduría") is an independent institution overseeing the public conduct of officials occupying public office and exercising a public mandate, thus overseeing the correct functioning of government institutions and agencies. The Procuradoría is not a judicial institution. It is mandated to safeguard the rights of citizens, guarantee human rights protection and intervene in the name of the people to defend the public interest and is charge of preventing, investigating and sanctioning misconduct by politicians, public servants and in general persons exercising public duties (OECD, 2013a).

OECD findings suggest that certain characteristics of the system in Colombia can be, depending on the features of the cases, inefficient. Legal proceedings can be lengthy, due to a backlog of pending cases before the courts and a lack of resources or means to speed up proceedings. Sanctions imposed by the Contraloría and Procuraduría can help law enforcement, but lead to a risk-averse, compliance-focused approach by public procurement officials. To counter these inefficiencies, public sector actors, led by Colombia's central purchasing body, *Colombia Compra Eficiente* (CCE), take actions to educate suppliers and public procurement officials in their rights and obligations and empower them to conduct procurements in a more efficient and effective way, avoiding unnecessary disputes. This chapter considers ways in which the system of public procurement review and control in Colombia can be developed to enhance its results.

"Soft" tools like observations and hearings exist

The Colombian public procurement system is organised to allow bidders to submit comments and enable public-private dialogue, so as to solve issues and avoid legal action.

Before launching a public tender, procurement authorities publish a draft of the tender documents and provide potential bidders the opportunity to comment on them. Bidders may request changes to the financial and technical requirements to amend eventual discriminatory terms or reflect the reality of the supply market, and have the right to receive a reply. For example, Article 23 of Decree 1510/2013 specifies that each government agency should, in the case of public tenders, invite observations to the draft tender documents within a deadline of ten days.

Public authorities also hold hearings (*audiencias*) during the procurement process, for example to discuss the allocation of contract risks and to announce the award decision,[1] which aim to clarify doubts regarding the procedure and allow bidders to request changes or make comments. Bidders can submit observations on the way the procedure is run[2] and the evaluation outcomes, as well as on mistakes or omissions that other bids may have. Bids can be reviewed by other bidders and their defects can be challenged, so some bidders employ legal counsel to look for irregularities in other bids. The authority is obliged to respond to observations submitted and may change its position (for example, amend a decision) if it finds that the observations have merit.

These "soft", non-litigious methods are important tools for bidders, who get a first chance to present their views, and provide opportunities for speedy, inexpensive solutions of disagreements during the procurement procedure, without disrupting it. They allow authorities to fix any wrongdoing before a complaint reaches the courts and, especially where an irregularity is due to a mistake, they can point to an error that can be corrected. If the bidder's observation is inaccurate, a submitted observation provides the opportunity to give explanations and present the arguments for the authority's position; an adequate explanation may convince the supplier and prevent further action (OECD/SIGMA, 2010). However, it would be best if hearings were conducted on line (with bidders submitting comments and receiving answers electronically), in order to avoid bidders meeting each other and offering them opportunities to collude (OECD, 2014, p. 45).

Responses during the OECD fact finding on whether public procurement authorities accept the observations and change their decisions show that authorities may be reluctant to consider and accept suppliers' feedback, thus turning the stage of observations into a formality. Observations are more likely to be accepted in large-scale projects, which are more heavily scrutinised. It would be helpful if the stages of hearings and observations were viewed as an opportunity, rather than a formality, and used to reach a common understanding and avoid disputes.

In addition, it may be helpful if losing bidders were debriefed in a structured way by authorities. In Colombia, losing bidders have the opportunity to find out how the award decision was reached in the hearing where it is announced, but are not otherwise debriefed on how to improve their next offer. Some OECD countries find that debriefing bidders on the strengths and weaknesses of their bids builds trust that processes are conducted in a fair manner and encourages them to participate in future processes with better chances. To achieve these goals, the United Kingdom has institutionalised debriefing discussions with bidders (Box 4.2).

The options and conditions of pre-trial remedies limit real chances of resolving disagreements

Colombian law provides for two types of complaints procedures: pre-trial administrative complaints brought before the public procurement authority (*vía gubernativa*) and litigation before the administrative courts (*control judicial*). Both sets of complaints, administrative or judicial, can only be filed against "final" decisions, like the decision to start a procurement process and the decision to award the contract or declare the tender inconclusive. Prior decisions (including those which support the selection, like technical and legal assessments) are considered to be procedural (*decisiones de trámite*) and not subject to remedies. All defects of the process can be invoked when a final decision is challenged.

Box 4.2. **Verbal debriefing in the United Kingdom**

Regulations in the United Kingdom require departments to debrief candidates for contracts exceeding European Union procurement thresholds. They also recommend debriefing for contracts below the thresholds.

Debriefing discussions are held face to face, by telephone or videoconference, within a maximum of 15 days following the contract award. The sessions are chaired by senior procurement personnel who were involved in the relevant procurement.

The topics for discussion during the debriefing depend mainly on the nature of the procurement. However, the session follows a predefined structure. First, after introductions, the procurement selection and evaluation process is explained. The second stage concentrates on the strengths and weaknesses of the supplier's bids to improve their understanding. After the discussion, the suppliers are asked to describe their views on the process and raise any further concerns or questions. At all stages, it is forbidden to reveal information about other submissions. Following the debrief, a note of the meeting is made for the record.

Effective debriefing may reduce the likelihood of legal challenge if suppliers are thereby convinced that the process has been carried out correctly and according to rules of procurement and probity.

Source: OECD (forthcoming), *Compendium of Good Practices for Integrity in Public Procurement.*

The fact that prior decisions cannot be challenged separately can be disruptive, in that issues are not tackled as soon as they arise and cases of bidders, who may be lawfully either excluded or reinstated, are not dealt with in good time. To enable matters to be handled and corrected or explained as soon as they arise, and thereby increase the lawfulness and transparency of the procurement procedures, the European Union legal framework on public procurement remedies requires decisions to be reviewed as quickly as possible at each stage of the procurement process (Box 4.3).

The only administrative complaint (*vía gubernativa*) available to bidders before the conclusion of the procurement contract is against the decision of the procurement authority to declare the tender inconclusive and not award the contract (*declaración de desierto del proceso*), called a "reconsideration" remedy (*recurso de reposición*). By this remedy, the bidder would seek a new decision by the procurement authority to award the contract to it.

The award decision itself cannot be challenged through an administrative complaint[3] and is only open to an annulment action before the courts. A bidder may request that the procurement authority revokes the award decision (*revocación directa*), but this is possible only in exceptional circumstances, for example when the award of the contract manifestly breaches the constitution or the law or is against public interest or causes unjustified damages.[4] Therefore, this remedy does not often succeed, as the conditions are hard to meet and would require an admission by the administration of a substantial mistake.

Box 4.3. The EU legal framework on public procurement remedies

The European Union has adopted two Directives laying down remedies in relation to public procurement: Directive 89/665/EEC, which covers the public sector; and Directive 92/13/EEC, which covers the utilities sector. Both Remedies Directives were amended by Directive 2007/66/EC.

The Remedies Directives require, as regards contracts falling within the scope of the Directives laying down substantive rules on public procurement (Directive 2004/17/EC and Directive 2004/18/EC, as replaced by Directive 2014/23/EU, Directive 2014/24/EU and Directive 2014/25/EU), that decisions taken by contracting authorities or contracting entities may be reviewed effectively and, in particular, **as quickly as possible**, on the grounds that such decisions have infringed EU public procurement law.

EU member countries may, in accordance with their national legal systems, limit the right to remedies in the following cases, for example:

i) Suppliers that could not have been awarded the contract, for example because they lack the critical technical qualifications, may be denied the right to challenge the contract award.

ii) Suppliers that have not participated in the procurement procedure may not be allowed to challenge contract award decisions. The reason is that such decisions do not affect outsiders to the procurement procedure.

iii) Suppliers that have been excluded at earlier stages of the award procedure (for example at the selection stage) may not have standing to challenge decisions taken at later stages of the procedure (for example, the award decision). In particular with regard to the right to challenge the contract award decision, according to article 2a(2) of Directive 89/665/EEC, the right to remedies may be denied to those tenderers that have been informed by the procurement authority of the (prior) decision concerning their exclusion and that decision has either been challenged and found lawful or the time limit for challenging the decision has passed. The right to challenge the award decision may also be denied to those candidates that were informed by the procurement authority of the rejection of their applications prior to the notification of the contract award decision. The reason is that the contract award decision does not affect tenderers that have been previously and definitively excluded from the procurement process.

iv) Suppliers that remain in the award procedure may not be allowed to challenge at later stages of the procedure any defective decisions that may have been taken at earlier stages of the procedure (for example, at the selection stage).

v) Community groups, contractors' trade associations, subcontractors, environmental associations or other interested bodies may not have access to public procurement remedies.

For further information, see http://ec.europa.eu/growth/single-market/public-procurement/infringements/ remedies/index_en.htm (accessed 18 August 2015).

Source: OECD/SIGMA (2010), "Public Procurement Training for IPA Beneficiaries", Module F: Review and Remedies; Combating Corruption, www.sigmaweb.org/publications/46189707.pdf (accessed 11 August 2015).

Therefore, the options for bidders who would like to raise a formal administrative complaint before the procurement authority seem to be few and difficult to succeed. Since the administrative, non-judicial stage, may provide an opportunity to resolve disagreements, it would be useful if the conditions and options available to bidders were reconsidered. As this is likely to require legal amendments which may take time, it would be useful if, in the meantime, the prior observations and hearing stages were more effectively used. Any change in the pre-trial complaints would need to be considered together the observations and hearing stages, so that bidders are offered real chances of presenting their views and protecting their rights, without however being allowed multiple remedies over the same issues and risking disruption of procurement procedures.

Newly introduced rules aim to enhance interim protection

Bidders can lodge annulment actions ("*acción de nulidad*"/ "*acción de nulidad y restablecimiento del derecho*") against the following decisions issued by the procurement authorities:

- decision to launch the tender procedure
- decision to award the contract
- decision to declare the tender inconclusive and not award the contract.

As mentioned above, all other steps and decisions during the tender process (like the draft and final evaluation report) are not subject to remedies as they are considered to be procedural (prior) decisions.

The courts competent to hear these cases are the administrative judges, the administrative courts or the Council of State (third section, with nine judges), depending on the location, the level of the procurement authority (national or subnational) and the amount involved in the litigation.

In addition to annulment, the bidder who considers itself harmed because it was not awarded the contract can claim compensation, asking for the profits that it would have earned if the contract had been awarded to it (lost profits). In all events, after the contract is executed, the only legal remedy available to a losing bidder is to ask for compensation. This remedy, although sometimes used due to the hope of being awarded profits and recover the costs of bidding, is not effective, because of the difficulty of proving that the bidder would have won the contract. This to an extent implies second-guessing the procurement authority's commercial decision to choose one bid over another and is therefore hard to prove. Also, as explained below, proceedings may take a long time (many interviewees mentioned up to 15 years for damages cases, including all possible appeals) and can have significant legal costs.

In particular with regard to interim (temporary) protection of the bidders' rights, this is vital in procurement, because irreversible situations are easily created as soon as the contract is concluded and starts being performed. If there is no quick interim protection, by the time a final court decision is reached, the performance will have progressed or be completed, thus making it impossible to reverse the situation and correct the wrongdoing. Suppliers want to win a contract and make a profit as well as also enter a market, build their experience, raise their profile in the market, attract new potential clients and so forth. Interim relief can allow them fair chances of intervening quickly in a process and reinstate them in the procedure, if they were unlawfully excluded, or exclude other bids with defects, if they were unlawfully included.

Case law on the possibility to be granted interim measures existed in Colombia, but it was piecemeal. In 2011, Colombia adopted the new Code of Administrative Proceedings and Judicial Review (*Código de Procedimiento Administrativo y de Contencioso Administrativo*, CPACA[5]), which introduced interim measures (*medidas cautelares*) in Articles 229, 230 and 231. These provisions allow the judge of a case to order the necessary interim measures to protect and guarantee, in a provisional manner, the result of the proceedings and the effectiveness of the judgment, balancing the likelihood of breach, the risk of harm being caused and the interests at stake. The judge, depending on the type of contested act, the claims and his own assessment of the situation, can order interim measures that are preventive (to prevent harm), conservative (to maintain the situation), anticipatory (ordering partial or complete provisional satisfaction of the claims) and suspensive (to suspend the effect of a decision or the procurement process) (*medidas cautelares preventivas, conservativas, anticipativas o de suspensión)*.

In general, the legal framework in Colombia is comprehensive, although complex. The adoption of the CPACA made the rights, procedure and measures that can be ordered clearer and introduces some procedural innovations in allowing physical hearings, as opposed to purely written procedure before, so as to speed up proceedings. CPACA is a useful tool and the fact finding indicates that its adoption was welcomed by suppliers and lawyers. As it only applies since July 2012, it is still in its roll-out phase; suppliers and their legal advisors are still getting familiar with some of its rules.

The review system provides options for aggrieved bidders but allows excessive legal actions

In addition to the remedies mentioned above, Colombia's Constitution provides an action for the protection of fundamental constitutional rights when these are threatened or harmed by an action or omission of a public authority (*acción de tutela*). The action can be lodged before any judge who must give priority to it and issue a decision quickly. In the fact-finding interviews it was reported that, in the area of public procurement, tutela actions are relatively frequently filed claiming breach of the right to due process, for example, when a bidder could not participate due to the tender terms or was excluded from a procedure. Cases are decided in approximately ten days and judges often grant the protection, ordering public procurement authorities to act or refrain from acting in a certain way; they may also order the suspension of the procurement procedure. Tutela decisions can be appealed, at the last instance before the Constitutional Court of Colombia.

Tutela is an instrument that was not designed for, and does not aim to solve, procurement-related disputes. It is a subsidiary remedy to be used exceptionally in case a constitutional right is breached, under condition that there's no other legal action available. As the CPACA provides for courses of legal action, including interim measures, many interviewees suggested that the use of tutela actions is in some cases excessive and part of that litigation is unmeritorious or dilatory and can lead to projects being suspended for a long time, or stopped, without a real abuse of constitutional rights. It would be useful, and important, to train judges and the suppliers in this regard.

Contractual litigation is more frequent than the pre-award one

Litigation with public authorities on contract disputes is frequent and more usual than pre-award litigation. One of the possible explanations suggested in the fact finding is that public officials are not equipped with technical knowledge or are reluctant to make decisions to solve issues, so disagreements end up in litigation. Another possible explanation is that lack of an effective pre-award remedy system stops issues from being raised during the tendering process, only to become contract administration issues later on.

Certain decisions of the procurement authority during the performance of the contract are subject to remedies, the reconsideration remedy (*recurso de reposición*) and contractual remedy (*acción contractual*), under special public law rules applicable to some public contracts.[6] These rules grant special powers to the procurement authority, like the right to unilaterally interpret, amend or terminate the contract, declare the supplier forfeit (*caducidad*, which is an extreme remedy of early termination for material default by the supplier[7]) or impose contractual penalties. Contesting the exercise of these powers can be at the root of additional litigation between the parties. Fact finding suggests that authorities can be sometimes quick to "pull the trigger" and use some of those powers, while suppliers contest every time the use of the special powers, whether justified or not. In Colombia, public contracts are not governed by private contract rules only. In some OECD countries, public contracts, once entered into, are subject to the usual contracts rules and the public buyer has no special rights vis-a-vis the contractor. Some of these issues are expected to be clarified in a law including provisions amending rules on public procurement legal remedies, which is being drafted.

There are also conciliation and settlement options in contracts, which do not always seem to work well. The amicable settlement process (*amigable composición*), a mediation mechanism which can be included in the contract and aims to have disputes resolved by a panel chosen by the parties, has not fully taken off. Fact finding suggested that public authorities are not at ease in this process and that, since the decisions of the panel can be appealed, parties prefer not to rely on it and go to court.

Arbitration can be agreed as resolution mechanism for contract performance disputes[8] and can help to avoid court-related delays and ensure a more specialised procurement expertise.[9] The major pros of arbitration in Colombia are:

- **Duration**: Arbitration takes between one and two years, while litigation before administrative courts may take a lot longer, in some cases up to 15 years.
- **Expertise**: There are arbitrators with expertise in public procurement and complex projects.
- **Time management**: Arbitrators can dedicate a significant amount of time to one arbitration, while administrative judges have a very large number of cases to decide.

Its major con is that arbitration tends to be more expensive than litigation before the courts, so may be best suited to big complex projects which may make the investment worthwhile. It is in fact common practice in large public works contracts and specialised projects. Also, arbitration is still rather long, as it has a series of procedural steps to set up the arbitral tribunal and carry out the proceedings.

Specialised public procurement tribunals, mentioned below, would handle contractual disputes. The pros and cons of setting one up in Colombia would need to be assessed, including budget and costs, resources and staffing, and any necessary legal amendments. The regime of special powers may need to be considered too, to check whether all aspects of it are necessary as opposed to a standard private (civil) contract.

The workload of the courts causes delays and limits the efficiency and effectiveness of the review system

Various stakeholders (associations of suppliers, lawyers as well as public authorities) reported to the OECD that bidders use the remedies available to them and trust court decisions. However, there are challenges in the review system of Colombia that may hinder its effectiveness. They include the significant workload of the courts, which results in delays in case handling and rendering judgments, the overall length of proceedings and the associated legal costs. The workload is due to lack of sufficient resources at the level of the courts, as well as, in some cases, litigiousness on the part of suppliers (who may start proceedings, even if their case is not strong or lacks merit, to delay procedures or force public authorities to abandon them) as well as public authorities (who avoid reaching consensual decisions), which adds to the number of pending cases. These challenges have been recognised, and a draft bill to amend the applicable regulation includes an article designed to reorganise cases and speed up the litigation process.

The Council of State attempts to decide on applications for interim measures within two weeks. In the fact finding, lawyers and suppliers reported that it usually takes much longer. In the case of the annulment actions, most interviewees concurred that the first instance proceedings for the main action (not interim measures) may take between two and five years and the appeal another two years at least (certain reported eight years in some cases). Following the adoption of CPACA, efforts are being made to speed up the process and the Council of State expects to have final judgments in two years. The length of proceedings increases in many cases legal costs and is a disincentive to using remedies, in particular for small and medium-sized enterprises (SMEs), who tend to have limited financial resources.

Enhancing resources available to the courts in Colombia would help. It may also help to consider alternative dispute bodies, like a specialised public procurement tribunal to deal with pre-award disputes, and possibly contractual ones, too. Since length of legal proceedings is a challenge faced in most OECD countries, some of them have set up special public procurement tribunals to help provide speedy expert resolution of disputes. Box 4.4 summarises some of the pros and cons of courts and specialised procurement tribunals.

Box 4.4. **Public procurement cases in courts and in specialised procurement tribunals**

The pros and cons of choosing the courts or a specialised procurement tribunal to handle public procurement cases may be summarised as follows.

Courts

Pros: Courts may have a better knowledge of general law and a broader experience in different laws, sectors and cases. Also, they are usually better acquainted with methods of interpretation and legal principles and more knowledgeable in applying them.

Cons: The procedure before the courts tends to take longer, as they also hear other cases. Usually there are no special procedural rules for procurement cases, so any inefficiency, like delays, of the judicial system will carry on. Also, they may lack specialised public procurement knowledge.

Specialised procurement tribunals

Pros: The procedure in specialised procurement tribunals is usually simpler as well as quicker, since they have to deal exclusively with procurement cases. They tend to be more aware of the realities of procurement and more familiar with procurement procedures and related issues.

Cons: The specialised tribunals may not be very familiar with the general law or legal principles on which procurement rules are usually based, and this may raise "correct" legal interpretation issues. Also, tribunal decisions need to be binding and enforceable in order for them to have real impact.

Source: Adapted from OECD/SIGMA (2010), "Public Procurement Training for IPA Beneficiaries", Module F: Review and Remedies; Combating Corruption, www.sigmaweb.org/publications/46189707.pdf (accessed 11 August 2015).

The members of a specialised procurement tribunal may include, in addition to persons with legal qualifications, persons with sector-specific background, like engineering or procurement project management. In appointing specialised persons, it is important to avoid conflicts of interests in the selection of members.

Germany and Slovenia have such specialised procurement tribunals (Boxes 4.5 and 4.6).

Box 4.5. **Specialised public procurement tribunals in Germany**

The review system in Germany applies to public procurement procedures covered by the EU public procurement directives. Complaints related to public procurement up until the award of the contract are, in the first instance, heard by specialised administrative procurement tribunals (*Vergabekammern*). At state (regional) level (*Länder*), there are regional procurement tribunals competent for procurement procedures under the responsibility of the Länder. At the federal level, there is a procurement tribunal with two chambers (due to workload) within the German competition authority, the Federal Cartel Office (*Bundeskartellamt*). All procurement tribunals are established in accordance with Part IV ("Award of Public Tenders") of the Act against Restraints of Competition (*Gesetz gegen Wettbewerbsbeschränkungen*).

There are three members of the chambers of the federal procurement tribunal. Two members (the Chair of the chamber and one member) are civil servants, appointed by the President of the Bundeskartellamt, following a job opening and an interview, for five years; this period can be renewed several times. The Chair must be qualified to be a judge, and usually the member has also a legal background. The third member is proposed by associations of suppliers and is a person experienced in public procurement, usually not a lawyer but an expert in technical issues.

The organisational structure of the procurement tribunals is similar to that of a court of law.

Litigants pay fees to cover the costs and expenses of the tribunals. Fees are at least EUR 2 500 and do not exceed EUR 50 000. Fees up to EUR 100 000 can be asked in cases where the commercial relevance, or the effort of the tribunal, is exceptionally high. The public procurement tribunal usually asks for a down payment of EUR 2 500 in order to proceed with the case. The winning party of the case may be awarded legal costs by the losing party.

The tribunal is not bound by the applications. If it finds that the case has merit, it may order suitable measures to remedy a situation and prevent further harm and can also request to suspend the procurement procedure.

The procedure before the tribunal is technical, facts-based, but with procedural safeguards to ensure the rights of due process. Decisions are rendered within five weeks; an additional two weeks may be allowed in exceptional cases.

Decisions of all procurement tribunals are binding. They can be appealed before the competent courts of appeal (*Oberlandesgerichte*); court proceedings can last six months or longer.

Source: Information provided by Bundeskartellamt. See also www.bundeskartellamt.de/EN/Publicprocurement/publicprocurement_node.html (accessed 14 August 2015).

Box 4.6. **The National Review Commission in Slovenia**

The review body in Slovenia for procurement-related disputes up until the award of the contract is the National Review Commission for Reviewing Public Procurement Award Procedures (the National Review Commission, *Državna revizijska komisija*). The National Review Commission can annul decisions of authorities in pre-award and award stages and can also guide authorities on how to implement its decisions.

The National Review Commission consists of five members appointed by the Parliament. Twelve experts support the work.

Filing fees vary between EUR 1 000 and EUR 25 000.

When all procedural requirements are fulfilled, the National Review Commission must render a decision within 15 working days from receipt of the claim and all necessary documentation. The 15 working days deadline can be extended, when this is justified, for a maximum of another 15 working days.

In Slovenia, statistics show that 83% of complaints are against the award decision, while the remaining 17% are against earlier decisions, for example alleging discriminatory requirements in the tender documents.

Source: Information provided by Public Procurement Directorate, Ministry of Public Administration, Slovenia. See also www.dkom.si/eng/ (accessed 18 August 2015).

Control mechanisms risk creating a compliance-focused approach to procurement decisions

The control system in Colombia relies on two independent control entities, the Contraloría and the Procuraduría.[10]

The Contraloría checks the legality of the steps of execution of the public budget, audits the accounts of public authorities and can open investigations into irregularities. The Contraloría has the roles attributed to supreme audit institutions:

- auditing oversight, to oversee the fiscal management of public funds
- liability oversight, to establish where responsibility lies in fiscal management and impose financial sanctions as necessary.

The Contraloría has 4 300 employees: 2 300 in Bogota and 2 000 in the capitals of the 32 Colombian regions. At the territorial level (in districts, departments and municipalities), control is carried out by the territorial Contralorías.

In public procurement, the entity uses its general powers, as there are no subject-specific rules or powers. If the Contraloría identifies irregularities in public procurement, it issues a report which may include fiscal, disciplinary and criminal findings. Depending on these findings, one or more of the Colombian external control institutions may be required to intervene. If there is an issue of fiscal mismanagement, the Contraloría can impose financial penalties, for which the relevant official is personally liable. If there is a finding of disciplinary responsibility, the Procuraduría will be called upon to assess the issue and impose a sanction. If there is a finding indicating the possibility of criminal activity, i.e. it is a criminal code issue, the Office of the Attorney General of Colombia

(*Fiscalía General de la Nación*), which belongs to the judicial branch of government, will assess the facts and take action. In fact, the same case could lead to three different procedures.

Contraloría's report is shared at draft stage with the relevant authority, which has a deadline to respond to the report and submit observations. The Contraloría takes into account the observations in its findings. If there are fiscal findings and improvements are required, the audited authority shall develop a roadmap to improve its practices. The monitoring of the plan's implementation is conducted by the audited authority's internal control office, and the Contraloría follows up to see if the recommendations are being put to practice. This collaborative process of developing recommendations is a good tool for improving public funds management practices.

The other control entity, the Procuraduría, exercises, in accordance with the Constitution, three types of actions: preventive, intervention and disciplinary.

- In its preventive role, the Procuraduría supervises public employees' performance and issues warnings if there are facts/behaviour that may violate rules or procedures. Preventive actions do not imply co-management.
- The intervention role enables the Procuraduría to intervene in legal proceedings, to defend legal order, the public interest or fundamental human rights.
- Under the disciplinary role, the Procuraduría is in charge of initiating, developing and ruling on investigations against public officials or any individual who exercises public functions or manages public resources, in accordance with Colombia's Disciplinary Code (Law 734 of 2002). The Procuraduría can impose disciplinary sanctions.

There are 32 regional Procuradurías with competences related to the public employees in departments and 52 provincial Procuradurías with competences over municipalities. At local level there are two additional institutions which carry out the responsibilities of the Procuraduría: the Personeros and the Veedores.

In public procurement, the Procuraduría studies tender documents, participates in the hearings and shares (legal, not technical) observations. The Procuraduría intervenes at its discretion (which could be prompted by a request, or on its own initiative) to ensure that the procurement process satisfies needs. It can order preventive measures without interfering with the procurement outcomes and share recommendations which can be adjusted by the relevant procurement authority. It also provides training.

The Procuraduría identifies its preventive role as its key role,[11] and more likely to have an impact in procurement than its disciplinary role to impose sanctions on public officials. Preventive action ensures that needs are satisfied, while disciplinary actions are taken after the fact, and can only punish wrongdoing, but not change it.

Disciplinary decisions include fines (for which the relevant official is personally liable with his own property) as well as striking an official from public service for up to 20 years.[12] Such decisions are subject to judicial control.

Fact finding shows that the Contraloría and the Procuraduría are active in public procurement. In order to fulfil their tasks, the two entities consult the information on SECOP (*Sistema Electrónico de Contratación Pública*) or may request CCE for additional data; they also consult any other source (including the media). The Contraloría's risk matrix does not use the red flags of SECOP, as the two systems do not interface (PwC EU Services, 2013). CCE provides the information requested and has, in addition, provided procurement data to the Procuraduría to help it construct the index called INTEGRA, a preventive control tool. The two entities are in regular contact with CCE to share views and ways to tackle issues, and take into account the agency's observations when they issue recommendations. They have participated in the trainings organised by CCE and have also received special training by it.

Interviewees submitted that CCE is a high performing entity that has improved procurement governance and operations, being both skilled at understanding sound procurement and capable of spreading this knowledge. It would be very helpful if the entity continues to work closely with Procuradoría and Contraloría to provide guidance and training and reinforce their role as strategic partners, supporting early problem identification and resolution, rather than *ex post* law enforcers with a punitive role.

The OECD fact finding showed that suppliers and their associations[13] may alert the two control entities to perceived irregularities in a procurement procedure and request their intervention to enforce the law. Interviewed associations also indicated that, when they are informed of concerns and suggestions in relation to a procurement procedure by one of their members, they would assess the merit of each case and, if found to be worthy of action, they would take it up with the procurement authorities, as well as with the control entities. The reason is to prompt immediate action and compel corrective measures by public procurement authorities, taking into consideration that court procedures are not quick. The two entities are not obliged to respond to requests and, due to limited resources, do not. They make an independent assessment of whether the case is worth acting on to ensure that the law is applied, not to protect the rights of bidders, though this may be a consequence of their action.

The procurement authority and/or the bidders may also request the two control entities' support during the procurement procedure ("*acompañamiento*"). This has been effective and helpful in some cases. Following instructions from the oversight bodies increases certainty that the law is complied with and limits the risk of personal liability. The support of the control entities does not interfere with the final outcome of a tender process; it consists in pointing out possible irregularities and warning the public officials of the fiscal and disciplinary consequences if they violate the law.

Fact finding suggests that the involvement of the two control entities in procurement can be useful in correcting irregularities but, at the same time, it can be narrowly focused on the law. In particular, given that procurement involves the taking of decisions on the choice of bidders and bids, which are to an extent discretionary, strict control combined with the risk of high personal liability may discourage officials and lead them to focus on formal compliance rather than on making commercially sound decisions. This can be exacerbated by the fact that there are no procurement-specific audit and control rules, which means that the scope of interventions by the control entities are not clearly delimited and can be far reaching.

In this respect, the OECD Recommendation provides that countries should "develop a system of effective and enforceable sanctions for government and private-sector procurement participants, **in proportion to the degree of wrongdoing to provide adequate deterrence without creating undue fear of consequences or risk aversion** in the procurement workforce or supplier community" (emphasis added).

The OECD found that public officials fear potentially high personal liability and are more concerned with avoiding it than in achieving good commercial results. Thus, they concentrate on complying with formal requirements and not on the efficient management of public procurement. They, in fact, prefer to have and follow formal rules and guidelines on when and how to act, rather than make their own decisions and risk being found wrong. Many interviewees, including lawyers and suppliers' associations, mentioned that officials follow long-established procedures, without examining their usefulness or appropriateness. Even if some rules allow flexibility, officials may lack confidence to use it, as they don't know how to, or are not used to, or are afraid they may make a mistake, thus missing opportunities to make procurement less cumbersome. The system seems to create "fear of consequences or risk aversion" in the sense of the OECD Recommendation. Interviewees reported that due to a combination of real risks and little rewards, careers in the public sector are less attractive for young people.

It would be recommendable to promote reasonable use of control by oversight entities, through:

- Assessing and eliminating any duplication in their powers. Some consideration can be given to reducing the personal liability of officials.[14]
- Training them on how to best use their role to promote good commercial results, while making sure that procurement procedures are fair, transparent and successful.
- Reinforcing their preventive (Procuradoría) and support for improvement (Contraloría) powers.
- Maintaining and enhancing joint work with CCE.
- Establishing an efficient remedy system, which will limit reliance on control mechanisms.

Professionalising and empowering the public procurement workforce

The fact finding showed that the key challenges in Colombia, in procurement in general and in the area of prevention and good management of disputes (whether pre-award or contractual) in particular, lay in reinforcing the knowledge and skills of the procurement workforce. Also, procurement legislation, while comprehensive, is highly complex and can lead to lack of clarity and inconsistencies in bidding practices, overly complicated procedures, a high number of supplier disqualifications and difficulties in contract interpretation and administration, which make procurement challenging for both suppliers (in particular SMEs) as well as the procurement workforce.

Not all authorities in Colombia currently have the resources, skills or motivation to be effective managers of procurement procedures or to implement and achieve public goals in general. The knowledge and powers required for effective management may exist, but are often dispersed throughout the public sector and not properly and cohesively co-ordinated within each single authority. Procurement knowledge is not systematically shared across the procurement authorities, and officials are not provided with guidance on how to capture it.

Lack in capability (knowledge and skills) or in capacity (number of procurement officials) of the public procurement workforce was identified as the most prominent weakness in the public procurement systems of OECD countries, as shown in Figure 4.1.

Figure 4.1. **Most prominent weaknesses identified in OECD member country procurement systems**

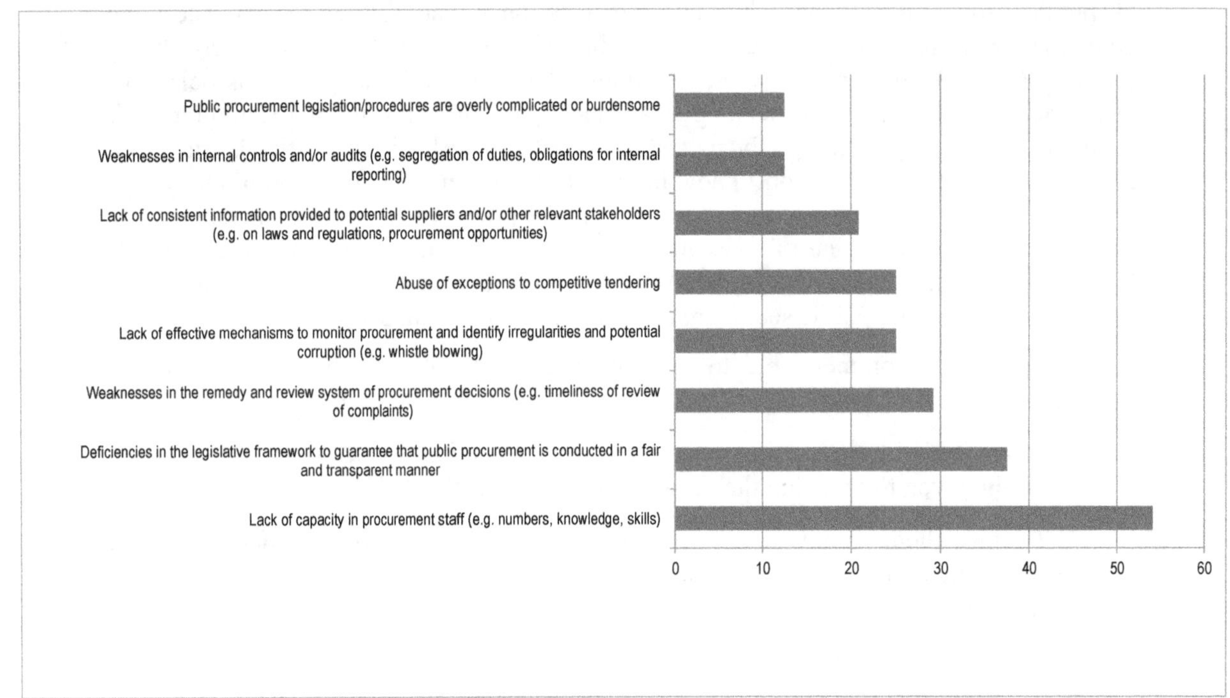

Source: OECD (2011), "Survey on progress made in implementing the OECD Recommendation on Enhancing Integrity in Public Procurement", OECD internal document.

In this regard, the OECD Recommendation provides that countries should "develop a procurement workforce with the capacity to continually deliver value for money efficiently and effectively". In particular, countries should "ensure that procurement officials meet high professional standards for knowledge, practical implementation and integrity by providing a dedicated and regularly updated set of tools, for example, **sufficient staff in terms of numbers and skills, recognition of public procurement as a specific profession, certification and regular trainings**, integrity standards for public procurement officials and the existence of a unit or team analysing public procurement information and monitoring the performance of the public procurement system" (emphasis added).

Enhancing the public procurement professional standards in Colombia requires empowering officials with the right skills (including technical knowledge and behavioural abilities) and authority, to allow them to run better procurement procedures and prevent gaps in planning, communication, tender choices and contract management that may lead to a complaint being raised in the first place. A skills-based procurement workforce with sufficient decision-making power has increased confidence and would be more likely to make and implement decisions in the public interest, including resolving disagreements in an amicable common-sense manner. It would thus be important to train public officials in Colombia in procurement competencies and management skills, instil confidence in decision making and change the perception that procurement is a formulaic administrative process.

To ensure the professionalism of the procurement workforce, many countries train and certify their procurement officials. For example, the Certification Program for the

Federal Government Procurement and Materiel Management Communities of the Canadian federal government aims to raise the professional standards of procurement (as well as materiel management) and recognise it as a knowledge-based profession (Box 4.7).

Box 4.7. **The Canadian Certification Program for the Federal Government Procurement and Materiel Management Communities**

In today's rapidly changing environment, the Canadian Federal Government's Procurement and Materiel Management Communities become a more knowledge-based profession, with an emphasis on a strategic advisory role. In an environment where accountability is foremost, it is essential that practitioners demonstrate they possess the advanced skills and knowledge required to function effectively and efficiently.

The Program is managed by the Acquired Services and Assets Sector (ASAS) Communities Management Office (CMO) in Treasury Board Secretariat. The CMO provides strategic direction and central leadership for the collaborative development and implementation of strategies, programmes and initiatives to support capacity building, community development and the professional recognition of the Federal Government Procurement, Materiel Management and Real Property Communities.

When the Certification Program was launched in 2006, it received national and international recognition as the Federal Government's first ever **Certification Program** for Procurement and Materiel Management specialists. What binds together the procurement and materiel management communities is their responsibility for the lifecycle management of assets, from assessment and planning of requirements throughout acquisition until disposal. As a consequence of this shared responsibility, the communities have many common competencies, learning goals and knowledge requirements.

Certification provides the increased professional recognition for the communities and offers a professional designation to formally acknowledge a practitioner's level of achievement. Procurement specialists can acquire certification as a Certified Federal Specialist in Procurement, Level I and II, and those in materiel management can acquire certification as a Certified Federal Specialist in Materiel Management Level I. Both designations are based on the Federal Government Procurement and Materiel Management Communities Competency Suite. A competency describes an employee's proficiency in a particular job function in terms of knowledge, skills and abilities. Each competency has a definition, a proficiency level and behavioral indicator statements.

The Certification Program is designed to evaluate a candidate's experience and knowledge in the federal government context, thereby distinguishing it from designations from external certifying bodies. In addition to developing technically proficient communities, the Program also focuses on ensuring capacity in leadership competencies.

Source: Information provided by Lorna Prosper, Director General, Defence Procurement and International Cooperation Embassy of Canada in the United States, Public Works and Government Services Canada. Also see www.tpsgc-pwgsc.gc.ca/ongc-cgsb/certification/index-eng.html (accessed 12 August 2015).

New Zealand has also put initiatives in place to build the knowledge and skills of its procurement workforce (Box 4.8).

Box 4.8. **Key initiatives to professionalise and empower the public procurement workforce in New Zealand**

Key initiatives to professionalise and empower the public procurement workforce in New Zealand include:

- Develop a model to assess the capability of procurement in agencies.
- Assess agency procurement capability on site and provide action plans for development.
- Agencies not targeted for onsite assessment complete a self-assessment against the procurement capability model.
- Develop standard procurement role competency requirements and implement in agencies.
- Benchmark key agency procurement and price performance against the private sector.
- Increase migration of skilled and qualified procurement professionals to fill skills gap.
- Ensure Government procurement salaries reflect market norms.
- Agencies to allocate resources to reform procurement practice.
- Identify opportunities for procurement shared service centres.
- Include procurement professionals in works project teams.
- Establish a small team of strategic procurement experts (Commercial Pool) to support high risk/ value projects across Government.
- Establish resource to support Public-Private Partnership projects.
- Determine procurement training needs and source providers.
- Agencies to use tools provided to assess procurement capability and capacity.
- Agencies to ensure procurement staff are trained to fill skill gaps identified.
- Provide e-learning to support procurers to gain a professional procurement qualification.
- Target key procurement personnel within agencies to fast track their professional procurement education.
- Develop and launch career development plans for procurement personnel.
- Develop New Zealand procurement academy.
- Encourage and subsidise public sector procurement professionals in gaining recognised procurement qualifications.
- Launch procurement graduate programme to increase New Zealand capacity.
- Facilitate secondments and career progression planning between agencies for procurement professionals.
- Establish and facilitate a Procurement Leaders Group (aged under 35 years) of future procurement leaders.
- Development of "Demystifying Procurement" as a two-day introductory course to procurement in a public sector context or alternatively for learning on line.

Source: Information provided by New Zealand Government Procurement, Ministry of Business, Innovation and Employment. Also see www.business.govt.nz/procurement/for-agencies/nz-procurement-academy.

It is equally important to make officials aware of their importance in safeguarding public interest and build their leadership skills, beyond the strict scope of procurement. The United Kingdom's National Health Service (NHS) has created a centre of excellence and best practice on leadership development for personnel from all backgrounds and experience, including but not focused only on, procurement (Box 4.9).

Box 4.9. **The United Kingdom's NHS Leadership Academy**

The United Kingdom's National Health Service (NHS) has created a centre of excellence and best practice on leadership development, the NHS Leadership Academy. Its mission is to develop leadership in healthcare through a set of national programmes to combine successful leadership strategies from international healthcare, private sector organisations and academic experts.

The Academy´s programmes take a multidisciplinary approach. They do not focus on enhancing procurement capabilities but rather provide, for each level of leadership responsibility in the NHS, targeted development for NHS personnel from all backgrounds and experience levels who have what it takes to create a more capable and compassionate healthcare system. The programmes aim to build essential leadership skills and support continuing development.

Source: NHS Leadership Academy's website, www.leadershipacademy.nhs.uk (accessed 13 August 2015).

In particular in the case of disputes, in order to both prevent them as well as tackle them efficiently, it is helpful to make officials more business-oriented and better acquainted with the commercial aspects of procurement. Procurement authorities and officials should be familiar not only with the procurement rules but also with public sector capacity (in terms of available human and material resources, and skills) and the supply market. Familiarity with this "operating environment" (law, capacity, the market) would provide a framework in which the public sector can work together with supplier to achieve realistic goals, rather than engage in disputes. The National Infrastructure Agency (*Agencia Nacional de Infraestructura*, the entity in charge of national-scale infrastructure projects through public-private partnerships) reported, for example, that they have managed to settle disputes totally or partially, as their purpose is not to win lawsuits but to reach an agreement to continue with the work.

Gaps in capacity in contract performance in particular were often brought up in the OECD fact finding. In this respect, it is, first, very useful to have model contracts to be used by all authorities, at least for standard purchases, with clear risk management tools for usual contract risks, dispute resolution mechanisms and designated persons on either side (public and private) to manage the contracts and related disputes. New Zealand, for example, has developed model contracts (Box 4.10).

Box 4.10. **Government model contracts in New Zealand**

The New Zealand Ministry of Business, Innovation and Employment (MBIE) has developed a set of standard conditions of contract for routine government purchases. These conditions are called government model contracts (GMCs).

The 2nd Edition GMCs were launched by MBIE in October 2011, replacing the 1st Edition GMCs that were launched in July 2010.

The development and implementation of GMCs is part of the Government Procurement Reform Programme and has been mandated by a Cabinet Directive requiring MBIE to "… create a standard, simple, plain English set of conditions of contract for common goods and services to be used by all Public Service Departments and State Services."

The GMCs are aimed at low-value, low-risk common goods and services. They have been designed as the default government contract. It is up to each agency using the GMCs to determine what constitutes low-value, low-risk common goods and services. This definition is subjective and will depend on the size of the agency and the scale and complexity of its procurement function.

Through the use of GMCs across the Public Service and State Services, Government aims to:

- provide simple, plain English contracts that are easy to use for both agencies and suppliers
- provide a fairer balance of risk between buyer and supplier
- standardise the treatment of legal risk in low-value, low-risk contracts
- reduce the need for negotiations and legal advice in routine purchases
- promote consistent practice across government
- promote process efficiencies in high-volume, low-value transactional contracting
- simplify doing business with government
- support improved procurement practice and align with international best practice.

Source: Information provided by New Zealand Government Procurement, Ministry of Business, Innovation and Employment. Also see www.business.govt.nz/procurement/for-agencies/government-model-contracts#Background.

The management of contracts requires not only technical skills but also understanding the project purposes and decision-making capacity to face issues that may arise during the performance. Examples of tools for successful supplier management are mentioned in Box 4.11.

Box 4.11. **Tools for successful supplier management**

Successful supplier management can rely on tools like:

- an open collaborative relationship with the supplier
- realistic expectations and timeframes agreed in advance
- good communication and mutual understanding of needs
- embedded safety and risk management processes
- defined escalation and dispute resolution procedures being in place
- embedded informal and formal reporting arrangements
- problems tackled immediately.

Source: Adapted from a presentation made at the OECD workshop on "Improving Public Procurement Practices in ISSSTE", 2-4 September 2014, Mexico City, by Steve Graham, Hadley Graham Ltd, advisors to the United Kingdom's Department of Health.

Many interviewees considered that CCE can add value and take a leadership role in promoting the professionalisation of the procurement workforce and the standardisation of contracts and management processes. It has been providing training to officials on public procurement issues (in particular on SECOP and now on SECOP II) almost since its establishment. Its training outreach is growing. Almost every day a member of its staff gives a virtual training and there is a series of in-person trainings across the country. This is particularly useful in the regions, as interviewees mentioned lower skills and higher needs for support in local procurement. As these trainings are covered by its own personnel, if they increase in frequency and importance (which is likely, at least in the case of training on SECOP II and related support and advice to public authorities), strengthening CCE's in-house capacity by allocating more staff to it may need to be considered.

In parallel to capacity-building activities provided by CCE's personnel, external support could be sought by specialised trainers and certifying bodies in public procurement to develop a full training curriculum, and certify officials according to their roles and levels. National universities could be involved as partners to provide inputs in the training curriculum and carry out parts of the training. In this respect, the OECD Recommendation provides that countries should "**promote collaborative approaches with knowledge centres such as universities, think tanks or policy centres to improve skills and competences of the procurement workforce**. The expertise and pedagogical experience of knowledge centres should be enlisted as a valuable means of expanding procurement knowledge and upholding a two-way channel between theory and practice, capable of boosting application of innovation to public procurement systems" (emphasis added).

CCE is developing a plan for the competency and career development of public procurement officials. This corresponds to the OECD recommendation to "**provide attractive, competitive and merit-based career options for procurement officials**, through the provision of clear means of advancement, protection from political interference in the procurement process and the promotion of national and international good practices in career development to enhance the performance of the procurement workforce" (emphasis added).

Public procurement capacity-building can be extended to suppliers

Not all suppliers, in particular those new to a market, know and understand all their procurement-related rights. In Colombia, international suppliers in particular usually ask for local legal advice to navigate the complexity of the public procurement regulations and understand the requirements, since there are cases of competitive bids excluded over formalities.[15]

The accountability of procurement involves, among other things, bidders knowing their rights. The existence, conditions and deadlines of complaints and legal actions must be "fully disclosed to economic operators, so that they know their rights in advance and may make use of them at the appropriate times, within the deadlines and before the designated review bodies (OECD/SIGMA, 2010). In Colombia, bidders' rights, at least as regards complaints before the procurement authority, are expressly mentioned in the tender documents. Other than this, suppliers receive no training or guidance, and rely on advice by their lawyers and in-house procurement teams.

CCE has taken steps to develop tools which make public procurement information more transparent and accessible and are useful for suppliers. First of all, it has, since its establishment in 2012, set up a helpdesk where its staff reply to questions on procurement. The OECD fact finding shows that the helpdesk is considered to be very helpful by suppliers, their associations and their advisors.

CCE also issues guides and manuals on specific topics to enable suppliers and authorities to get procurement right. The drafts of such manuals and guides are published on line and comments, questions and suggestions are invited before they are finalised. The documents are then placed on line for free.[16] This collaborative development process has worked well. CCE has, in addition, developed videos on SECOP and the e-shop (*Tienda Virtual del Estado Colombiano*). Furthermore, to enable a common approach to issues of general procurement interest, CCE issues circulars which public entities have to follow. All these tools are monitored on an ongoing basis, to check if they need to be updated, for example following new relevant case law, or inputs by public authorities or private sector stakeholders.

An important tool CCE has developed to clarify and spread legal information is a free webpage called Síntesis, which contains public procurement rules and regulations, court judgments and arbitral awards, as well as summaries (*fichas*) of court judgments. Síntesis provides links to all related information (like all legal precedents on a matter), for those who wish to obtain full information on an issue. Filters allow visitors of the webpage to screen the information according to subject, title and type of information. Visitors can submit questions on line. Síntesis simplifies and clarifies technical legal information. As such, it facilitates access to information, increases awareness of the current state of the law and suppliers' rights under it and levels the playing field for suppliers and authorities, in particular SMEs and small authorities, which do not have the budget to have continuous legal support.

The OECD mission found that Síntesis is frequently consulted and is perceived as useful by suppliers (in particular SMEs), their associations and legal advisors, as well as the media. Lawyers and larger suppliers may use Síntesis but also rely on specialised legal databases for their legal research. Síntesis is gaining ground and it is expected that its relevance will increase over time, as people become familiar with it and consult it more. As it is prepared and fed by the in-house legal team of CCE, the team may in the future need reinforcement to be able to review all new information, summarise it in plain language and publish it quickly.

In addition to these tools, it would be helpful to conduct in-person and virtual training and guidance for suppliers, to familiarise them with the changing public procurement environment, tools like SECOP II, framework agreements and auctions, as well as their rights. Most capacity-building activities by CCE are for public authorities but could be extended to suppliers. Currently CCE conducts training sessions for public officials on the deployment of SECOP II across the country. It could combine these activities with parallel training sessions to local associations of suppliers on SECOP II as well as more general public procurement issues, guiding them on how to look for, find and apply for business opportunities with the public sector and make sure that they are not disqualified over formalities.

Recommendations

- Professionalising the public procurement workforce is a priority through regular trainings, certification and career development options. Targeted training to public procurement officials, on how to best use their role to promote good commercial results, would help to make them less risk-averse and more results-oriented.
- Trainings and guidance should be extended to suppliers and oversight bodies.
- The scope of procurement oversight should be clearer. There is need to assess any duplication in the tasks of oversight bodies. Powers as well as give some consideration to reducing the personal liability of officials for procurement-related mistakes.
- The stage of hearings and observations can be viewed as a real opportunity for mutual explanations to avoid disputes, rather than a formality. It would be best if these were conducted on line, in order to avoid bidders meeting each other and offering them opportunities to collude.
- Pre-trial complaints should be enhanced, and offer real possibilities of assessing and resolving disputes.
- Litigation is delayed as a result of the workload of the courts. A specialised public procurement tribunal may help, dealing with pre-award as well as contractual disputes. A law expected to improve dispute resolution is being drafted.

Notes

1. Article 9 of Law 1150/2007. In the allocation of risks hearing, the authority must submit a risks analysis (Article 39 of Decree 1510/2013).

2. Art 24.2 of Law 80 provides that bidders must be given the opportunity to raise comments during the public procurement procedures.

3. Paragraph 1 of Article 77 of Law 80 of 1993.

4. Article 93 of Law 1437/2011, the Code of Administrative Proceedings and Judicial Review (*Código de Procedimiento Administrativo y de Contencioso Administrativo*, CPACA).

5. Law 1437/2011.The law was developed over three years and was enriched by discussions with France, Germany and Costa Rica.

6. Law 80/1993, in particular Articles 14-18 and 77.

7. Under this remedy not only is the relevant contract terminated early, but also, automatically, all other public contracts that the supplier has. The supplier is also debarred from public procurement for five years. Many interviewees maintained that this remedy is neither useful nor proportionate: on the one hand, it does not get the contract performed and, on the other, it may bring about the supplier's bankruptcy.

8. Article 1 of Law 1563 of 2012.

9. In terms of numbers reported (not verified) in the fact finding, in arbitration cases public authorities have 24% rate of success against 90% in court cases.

10. General information on external control in Colombia in this section is based on OECD (2013b).

11. For more information, see www.procuraduria.gov.co/portal/Objetivos-y-funciones.page (accessed 17 August 2015).

12. Articles 44 to 47 of Law 734/2002, Disciplinary Code. Articles 44 to 60 of 1474 of 2011.

13. Interviewed suppliers' associations include the ACOPI (*Asociación Colombiana de las Micro, Pequeñas y Medianas empresas*, the association of SMEs), ANDI (*Asociación Nacional de Empresarios de Colombia*, the association of large companies), the Colombian Chamber of Infrastructure (*Cámara Colombiana de la Infraestructura*, the association of big and medium-sized construction companies and suppliers of infrastructure materials) and the *Sociedad de Ingenieros* (the association of engineers).

14. For example, in Canada, if it can be shown that officials are acting in good faith and within the boundaries and authority of their position, they are not personally financially liable, and are protected by the Crown (in policy).

15. It was mentioned in the fact finding that exclusion for legal formalities is more marked in smaller procurements where smaller, less qualified authorities are involved, as procurement officials are less confident to make decisions on technicalities.

16. The manuals and guides can be consulted at http://colombiacompra.gov.co/es/manuales-y-documentos-tipo and the circulars at http://colombiacompra.gov.co/es/circulares.

References

Botero Marino, C. (2002), "Acción De Tutela Contra Providencias Judiciales En El Ordenamiento Jurídico Colombiano", http://www.icesi.edu.co/precedente/ediciones/2002/1CatalinaBotero.pdf.

Mario, R. and C. Colpas (2012), "Analysis of the Precautionary Measures in the Colombian Administrative and Contentious Administrative Procedure law, from a Constitutional Perspective", *Advocatus*, Edición especial No. 18: 33-44, Universidad Libre Seccional, Barranquilla.

OECD (forthcoming), *Compendium of Good Practices for Integrity in Public Procurement.*

OECD (2016), *Improving ISSSTE's Public Procurement for Better Results*, OECD Public Governance Reviews, OECD Publishing, Paris, http://dx.doi.org/ 10.1787/9789264249899-en.

OECD (2015a), "Recommendation of the Council on Public Procurement", www.oecd.org/corruption/recommendation-on-public-procurement.htm.

OECD (2015b), *Government at a Glance 2015*, OECD Publishing, Paris, http://dx.doi.org/10.1787/gov_glance-2015-en.

OECD (2014), "Fighting Bid Rigging in Public Procurement in Colombia: A Secretariat Report on Colombian Procurement Laws and Practices", www.oecd.org/daf/competition/Booklet_SIC%20Procurement%20Report_16X23_REV_web.pdf.

OECD (2013a), *Implementing the OECD Principles for Integrity in Public Procurement: Progress since 2008*, OECD Public Governance Reviews, OECD Publishing, Paris, http://dx.doi.org/10.1787/9789264201385-en.

OECD (2013b), *Colombia: Implementing Good Governance*, OECD Public Governance Reviews, OECD Publishing, Paris, http://dx.doi.org/10.1787/9789264202177-en.

OECD (2011), "Survey on progress made in implementing the OECD Recommendation on Enhancing Integrity in Public Procurement", OECD internal document.

OECD/SIGMA (2010), "Public Procurement Training for IPA Beneficiaries", Module F: Review and Remedies; Combating Corruption, www.sigmaweb.org/ publications/46189707.pdf (accessed 11 august 2015).

PwC EU Services (2013), "Identifying and Reducing Corruption in Public Procurement in the EU", http://ec.europa.eu/anti_fraud/documents/anti-fraud-policy/research-and-studies/identifying_reducing_corruption_in_public_procurement_en.pdf (accessed 8 November 2015).

ORGANISATION FOR ECONOMIC CO-OPERATION AND DEVELOPMENT

The OECD is a unique forum where governments work together to address the economic, social and environmental challenges of globalisation. The OECD is also at the forefront of efforts to understand and to help governments respond to new developments and concerns, such as corporate governance, the information economy and the challenges of an ageing population. The Organisation provides a setting where governments can compare policy experiences, seek answers to common problems, identify good practice and work to co-ordinate domestic and international policies.

The OECD member countries are: Australia, Austria, Belgium, Canada, Chile, the Czech Republic, Denmark, Estonia, Finland, France, Germany, Greece, Hungary, Iceland, Ireland, Israel, Italy, Japan, Korea, Luxembourg, Mexico, the Netherlands, New Zealand, Norway, Poland, Portugal, the Slovak Republic, Slovenia, Spain, Sweden, Switzerland, Turkey, the United Kingdom and the United States. The European Union takes part in the work of the OECD.

OECD Publishing disseminates widely the results of the Organisation's statistics gathering and research on economic, social and environmental issues, as well as the conventions, guidelines and standards agreed by its members.

OECD PUBLISHING, 2, rue André-Pascal, 75775 PARIS CEDEX 16
(42 2016 05 1 P) ISBN 978-92-64-25208-0 – 2016

www.ingramcontent.com/pod-product-compliance
Lightning Source LLC
LaVergne TN
LVHW080929120826
845149LV00018B/1707
* 9 7 8 9 2 6 4 2 5 2 0 8 0 *